EXTRACT
VALUE
FROM **CONSULTANTS**

HOW TO HIRE, CONTROL, AND FIRE THEM

GORDON PERCHTHOLD | JENNY SUTTON

GREENLEAF
BOOK GROUP PRESS

Published by Greenleaf Book Group Press
Austin, TX
www.gbgpress.com

Distributed by Greenleaf Book Group LLC

For ordering information or special discounts for bulk purchases, please contact Greenleaf Book Group LLC at PO Box 91869, Austin, TX 78709, 512.891.6100.

Design and composition by Greenleaf Book Group LLC
Cover design by Greenleaf Book Group LLC

Content by Barbara Minto (chapter five) is used with permission.
Content by Geert Hofstede (appendix one) is used with permission.

Publisher's Cataloging-In-Publication Data (Prepared by The Donohue Group, Inc.)
  Perchthold, Gordon.
  Extract value from consultants : how to hire, control, and fire them / Gordon Perchthold [and] Jenny Sutton. -- 1st ed.

    p. : ill. ; cm.
  Includes bibliographical references and index.

  ISBN: 978-1-60832-035-6

1. Business consultants--Selection and appointment. 2. Business consultants--Rating of. I. Sutton, Jenny. II. Title.

HD69.C6 P47 2010
658.4/6   2010920230

Part of the Tree Neutral™ program, which offsets the number of trees consumed in the production and printing of this book by taking proactive steps, such as planting trees in direct proportion to the number of trees used: www.treeneutral.com

Printed in the United States of America on acid-free paper

10 11 12 13 14   10 9 8 7 6 5 4 3 2 1

First Edition

To our clients,
past, present, and future

CONTENTS

ACKNOWLEDGMENTS

OVER THE YEARS WE HAVE BEEN FORTUNATE TO WORK WITH A NUMBER of consulting partners who served as good role models in terms of serving clients, developing consultants, and building consulting practices. Two partners in particular stand out for both of us. Graham Baragwanath, who we worked with when he was the Managing Partner of the Toronto office of Deloitte Consulting from 1992 and later when he was Asia Regional Managing Partner, demonstrated unwavering integrity, was always focused on doing the right thing for the client, and provided us practical guidance over many years while we were with Deloitte. Robert Contri was a Senior Manager in the New York office of Deloitte Consulting when we first met him on a project in Cape Town in 1994 (he is now Senior Partner, Financial Services Consulting, in New York). We learned from him how to effectively combine content knowledge with consulting skills to deliver value for clients. Graham's and Robert's capabilities and commitment to the profession of consulting still serve as our benchmark.

A number of our family members, friends, and clients took the time to read early drafts and provide us feedback on the concept, contents, and messages. We are grateful to Mona Attard, Saskia Goedhart, Dave McKay, Peter Perchthold, Jon Sparks, Jessop Sutton, and Andreas Wilhelm for their valuable input and to all the others, including those in major consulting firms, who encouraged us in this endeavor.

Our fantastic publisher, Greenleaf Book Group, has been a breath of fresh air. Their enthusiastic personnel have fast-tracked activities in order to meet deadlines, provided us the control we desired, and treated us as valued customers.

And without the advice and direction of Sandy Diaz and Marissa Eigenbrood at Smith Publicity, who have been an immense help in guiding us through the ecosystem of players involved in bringing a book by new authors to market, this book would not have found its way into our readers' hands.

—Gordon and Jenny

TIME TO EVEN THE ODDS

GO AHEAD. LOOK AT THE BOOKS IN YOUR FAVORITE ONLINE OR PHYSICAL bookstore. You will see many books about how to be a management consultant. You might find a few books that tell you how bad consultants are. But there will be few, if any, books to help you, the private or public sector manager or employee, effectively select and manage consultants. So who do you think has the advantage?

We titled this book *Extract Value from Consultants* in recognition that it takes proactive effort on the part of the manager hiring consultants to obtain the value available from them. Too often, managers passively wait, relying on the consultant to identify what, where, and how they will deliver value. We have written this book to enable managers to maximize the value created by using consultants.

As shown in the figure on page 2, our careers began in the early 1980s—with technology vendors and the technology departments of large companies—before eventually gravitating to the management consulting industry. We have had a broad range of experiences on hundreds of client projects spanning multiple functional areas for dozens of prominent

Figure 1.1: Career and Geographic Background of Authors

	Gordon Perchthold		Jenny Sutton	
Toronto	B.Com(tions), University of Toronto		B.Com(tions), University of Cape Town	Cape Town
			Old Mutual	
	Unisys		Wooltru Computer Services	
		1985		
Melbourne			Mercantile & General	
Sydney			Zarab HR Computer Services	
			Hodge & Sutton Consulting	
Toronto	MBA, Ivey Business School	1990	Infomet Methodologies	
	NCR			
	Deloitte Consulting			
Cape Town			Deloitte Consulting	
New York			MBA, University of Cape Town	
Mexico		1995		Toronto
Toronto				Milwaukee
Sydney	Accenture			New York
New York	Deloitte Consulting			Columbus
Hong Kong				Zurich
Seoul		2000		Hong Kong
New York				Bangkok
Tokyo	ABeam Consulting			Tokyo
Taipei		2005		
Asia	The RFP Company			Asia

multinational companies across more than twenty countries in Asia, Australia, Europe, North America, and Africa. Although we come from opposite ends of the globe, our similar educational backgrounds integrate technology into the practice of business management. In the consulting field we have both worked extensively on business operations and process initiatives, though Jenny came at this from the technology angle and Gordon approached it from the business strategy perspective. Of course, all these initiatives have involved significant change management, and over the years we have grown to appreciate that the people issues are typically the biggest challenge to overcome in any project.

As we progressed up the consulting pyramid from senior consultants to partners within Deloitte Consulting (and, in Gordon's case, including a one year "sabbatical" at Andersen Consulting, now known as Accenture), we observed firsthand the evolution of the consulting profession. We were fortunate to have had good mentors in the early days of our careers who taught us about the profession of consulting, to improve the discipline in our thinking, and to put client needs first and foremost. While at Deloitte and Accenture, we were exposed, through temporary assignments or permanent relocations, to management consulting practices and clients around the globe allowing us to observe and participate in alternate approaches to solving problems, developing people, building consulting practices, and serving clients. But, as discussed in this book, the consulting industry, once a client-focused profession, was increasingly becoming a revenue-focused business. It also became evident to us that consulting firms' sales approaches have become remarkably sophisticated as the scale of consulting projects sold has rapidly ratcheted up. Yet buyers of consulting services did not appear to be getting any better at selecting and managing consultants.

As partners with Deloitte Consulting and later as managing partners of the International Client Services business unit of the Japanese spin-off of Deloitte Consulting, ABeam Consulting, we found that our time was increasingly spent in internal meetings attending to partnership structures, revenue planning, resource arbitration among partners, consultant performance evaluations, and administrative matters. Very little time was being spent on the activities we enjoyed most—serving our clients, developing skills in others, generating thought leadership, and structuring complex projects.

As a result, in 2006 we bade farewell to the large global consulting firms and established The RFP Company, a management consulting firm that focuses on enabling clients to make strategic choices. We now remain personally involved with every aspect of client service delivery. Our approach has been to apply concentrated expertise and experience while leveraging client personnel thus strengthening the organizational capabilities of our clients.

While selecting consultants on behalf of our clients, we have had extensive exposure to the sales tactics and delivery approaches of a wide variety of consulting firms and other vendors spanning strategy, process, technology, and outsourcing services. Too many buyers of consulting services are uninformed about what drives the consulting business; lack experience in executing a structured and disciplined request for proposal (RFP) process; are uninitiated when it comes to contracting, and do not spend enough time thinking about how to effectively structure projects. Thus, more than they may realize, they are easily influenced by consulting partners whose interests might not always align with theirs.

We decided to write this book to document our experiences and assist a much broader audience to secure better results from their use of consultants. The right type of consultants, used for the right reasons, have the potential to provide significant value to organizations in challenging and structuring thinking, overcoming the status quo, and turning ideas into actions. But management's lack of experience in effectively using consultants and the internal objectives within consulting firms often conspire against this outcome.

Poor value from consultants is often a direct result of poor selection and poor management of consultants. In this new economic era, organizations must be more prudent and extract more value from their expenditures on consultants.

Use This Book to Your Advantage

This book costs less than a few minutes with a partner from a typical global management consulting firm. Packed with experiences, case studies, checklists, and secrets of the consulting trade this book will potentially add hundreds of thousands to millions of dollars to the bottom line (depending on consulting spend) by allowing you to achieve better business outcomes while reducing fees and expenses simply by applying the principles to existing or new projects.

Throughout this book, the term "consultant" is used to collectively refer to people or organizations offering professional expertise—whether as a single consultant or as a group of consultants or consulting firms. We have used the term "individual consultant" when we are referring to an employee of a consulting firm and "independent consultant" to refer to sole practitioners. The term "consulting firm" is used when referring to consulting businesses, which are usually headed by partners or principals to deliver consulting services. In some countries, consulting firms are also referred to as consultancies.

Part I will explain the consulting business: the economic operating models for consultants, and how those influence the fees you pay; the culture inside the firms; and how the industry has evolved and proliferated into the consulting firms you see today. Understanding the levers that drive the revenues and profits of different types of consulting firms will allow you to access the appropriate resources and negotiate a fair price to achieve a defined business outcome. The discussion in this book is applicable to both private and public sector organizations; however, we will use the term "business" in the context of objectives and outcomes applicable to both types of organization.

Part II discusses typical pitfalls in defining the problem for consultants to work on, the danger of being hypnotized by brand and marketing, considerations for a well-structured RFP, reading between the lines of a consultant's proposal, approaches for making a selection that can be defended, and issues in contracting the right type of consultant. Throughout this section we reveal tricks of the consulting trade that will allow you to make more informed decisions in the future.

Part III will help you configure the consulting team and manage your consultants not only to deliver business benefits but also to strengthen your organization's internal capabilities. As part of the process, you will also learn how to break the ongoing cycle of new projects and wean yourself off consultants. Of course you, as the manager hiring the consultants, can have significant influence on the productivity and value delivered by consultants, so we highlight some of the unproductive practices we often see organizations inadvertently use that undermine their consultants' success.

The majority of global consulting firms originated in America or Western Europe. In Asia, the world's fastest-growing region, management consulting is a relatively new concept and has only been adopted more readily in the last decade or so. The competency and bench strength of the relatively immature consulting profession in Asia, even among the global consulting firms, is therefore significantly more variable than in Europe and North America so buyers must beware. Clearly, the capability of consultants in Asia is a concern for organizations based in Asia. But it should also be a concern for companies headquartered in other regions that are undertaking more and more initiatives that include Asia. Selection of consulting firms for these far-reaching programs should not be excessively biased by global branding or toward the handpicked consultants presented to global headquarters, but should consider actual capabilities in all key regions. Accordingly, no book on using consultants would be complete without addressing the additional challenges of selecting and working with consultants in Asia, as we have done in appendix 1.

The RFP itself is pivotal to the successful selection of consultants. It allows you to set the tone for the rest of the project, to define the rules of engagement, and to set out your expectations of the consultant. To aid you in the compilation of this document, we have provided a sample table of contents for a typical RFP in appendix 2.

The contract you write with your selected consultant will govern the relationship after the project starts. A balanced, comprehensive contract will ensure that the appropriate expectations are set on both sides and that the impact of future conflict and disagreements will be mitigated. Appendix 3 contains a list of the key components of a consulting contract.

Management checklists for evaluating your organization's ability to extract value from consultants as well as to evaluate the consultants themselves in terms of their propensity to deliver value can be found in appendixes 4 and 5, respectively.

Throughout this book we have used case studies to highlight the key messages within a chapter. These case studies have been drawn from a wide range of sources—primarily selection projects conducted on behalf of our clients, other consulting firms' concurrent projects at our clients, experiences relayed to us by others, and a couple of the projects we were involved in while with global consulting firms.

Consultants target their sales efforts to the most senior executives of an organization. To understand what drives the behavior and approaches of consultants these executives should ensure that they read part I so they improve their ability to consider the right types of consultants for the appropriate projects. If pressed for time, the management summaries at the end of each chapter in parts II and III, as well as the management checklists in appendixes 4 and 5, should also be reviewed to allow senior executives to familiarize themselves at a high level with the process and pitfalls when selecting, controlling, and releasing consultants. Project sponsors, selection team members, project managers, business managers, and project participants, however, will only become equipped to effectively manage consultants if they learn from the experiences, templates, and case studies discussed throughout the book across the different stages of the client-consultant relationship. We recommend reading the entire book before utilizing it to draft an RFP or finalize a contract as many of the activities subsequent to issuing an RFP and writing a contract should be considered in the RFP and the contract.

We hope that this book will help to even the odds for you when dealing with management consulting firms and to assist you to extract greater value from consultants in the future.

PART I

UNDERSTAND HOW CONSULTANTS
MAKE MONEY FROM YOU

CHAPTER 1

EXTRACTING VALUE NEED NOT BE DIFFICULT

CONSULTANTS ARE ABLE TO IMPROVE THE PERFORMANCE OF YOUR organization by applying deep domain expertise and broad project experiences in a structured way to solve problems and communicate solutions. But consultants often disappoint their clients. Based on the comments we have heard from many frustrated managers, consultants often fail to adequately deliver the solution to the original problem they were asked to address. In some cases, they focus on other problems instead, or worse, they create new ones.

Errors of Commission

Most likely you have also experienced this disappointment. How could this be possible? After all, you pay consultants considerable sums of money with the expectation that they will achieve specific, agreed-upon business objectives in return. Failure occurs for a number of reasons, some in combination, including the following:

- The consultants are working on the wrong problem either because you have not defined the problem clearly or they have persuaded you to allow them to work on something other than what you hired them for—usually something easier or that generates more fees.
- You have selected the wrong type of consultants for the problem at hand and therefore they do not have the domain knowledge, local presence, or industry expertise to determine the appropriate solution to the problem.
- The consultants do not have the skills or experiences that were proposed because of substitutions: the individual consultants with the credentials on which you based your selection decision have been replaced with less qualified people.
- You are not controlling or managing the consultants effectively so the consultants are running amok in your organization and/or the project is significantly delayed or over budget without you realizing it.
- The consultants have lost their effectiveness in your organization either because they are too familiar with you and have become part of your organization's groupthink, or they have been marginalized by your managers, thus blocking their meaningful participation.

Meeting Experience with Inexperience

Consultants are proficient at packaging their services, influencing decision makers in organizations, making a compelling sales pitch, and contracting to their advantage. They do it every day. They have an uncanny ability to realign themselves and redefine their services to secure work and protect partner income irrespective of the economic cycle. In 2008, when the most recent recession began—purportedly the worst since the Great Depression—global consulting revenues declined only 5.5 percent according to Kennedy Consulting Research and Advisory. Consulting indeed has become a big business. From its previous historic peak in 2008 of US$305 billion, by 2012 revenue is projected to have recovered from its minor dip to reach US$315 billion. To place that figure in context, the consulting industry will earn an average of about US$45 a year for every man, woman, and child on the planet! However, managers claim that they pay too much and get too little value from consultants. To a large extent this failure to realize value stems from a lack of knowledge on the part of the manager of how to effectively hire, efficiently control, and judiciously fire their consultants.

Because the decision to hire a consultant is highly decentralized in most organizations, the managers involved usually have significantly less experience structuring the relationship than the consultants do. To an experienced consultant, clients—the organization or individual using consultants—are often amateurs when it comes to dealing with them. Consultants target senior managers who they know have ambitious agendas, often struggle to effect change in their organization, have large budgetary authority, and can be easily persuaded by personable consultants and well-structured presentations to buy consulting services. Don't you think it's about time you evened the odds?

Consultants Are a Valuable Management Resource

Although this book may appear in places to be critical of the consulting profession, we do not intend to imply that all consultants engage in negative practices, and we are certainly not recommending that you simply avoid hiring consultants. On the contrary, consultants are indeed a valuable management resource for any organization. When the appropriate type of consultant is engaged for sound reasons and at a cost-justifiable fee, and if they are managed effectively, they will enable your organization to achieve benefits that would not have been achieved without them.

As our clients always remind us, every client's problem is slightly different. Therefore, we have not tried to compile a cookbook with the recipe for extracting value from consultants that would work perfectly every time. Rather, we have presented management principles that can be applied to most situations involving the selection, management, and termination of consulting services. And while we have discussed some of the legal and commercial aspects of the contract itself, any contract you conclude should reflect your specific situation and involve the appropriate legal review.

Structural Change Not Required

Many times, management books are based on a new business approach requiring you to change the structure of your organization or implement new technology in order to realize the benefits of the proposed approach (e.g., reengineering, customer relationship management, or balanced scorecards). This can be exceedingly difficult for organizations to do. This book is different. Your organization will continue to use consultants. No revolutionary changes or restructuring are required to increase your organization's effectiveness in doing so. Simply by becoming educated about the consulting business model, understanding what motivates consultants, and leveraging the principles contained within this book, your employees will become more adept at hiring, controlling, and firing consultants. This applies to the members of your executive committee who approve the hiring of consultants, the project sponsor and selection team who participate in the hiring process, the project manager who is managing the consultants, and your employees who are working or interacting with the consultants. You will see greater business results for lower consulting spend. The impact could be in the order of millions of dollars added to the bottom line—from something you are already doing!

Value Depends on You

In the final analysis, the failure to derive sufficient value for money from consultants is generally not the failure of the consultant. The failure is most likely yours. This book, which provides case studies, templates, checklists, and tricks of the trade based on more than fifty years' experience, will help you carry out your responsibility of extracting value from consultants.

Management Summary

- Consultants can potentially help organizations achieve greater performance levels—if organizations effectively manage them.

- The consulting industry extracts significant revenue from its clients—companies, governments, and nonprofit organizations. Although the experience of many managers is that they do not realize sufficient value for their expenditure, this often arises due to inexperience in selecting, managing, and releasing the consultants.

- Consultants engage as service providers with managers in client organizations every day. However, for these managers, engaging consultants is just one of the many aspects of their job, and something that they do not necessarily do on a regular basis. It is no wonder consultants often have the upper hand in the relationship.

- Understanding how the consulting industry works and each step of the consulting engagement process will allow managers to even the odds when they are dealing with consultants.

CHAPTER 2

HOW CONSULTANTS ADD VALUE

GIVEN THE OFTEN-VOICED DISSATISFACTION WITH THE CONSULTING profession, it is a wonder that anyone actually hires consultants. But organizations do hire them because consultants are an important management resource. However, one of the reasons managers may be dissatisfied is that they do not always consciously define their requirements nor do they explicitly state their reasons for engaging a consulting firm. The result is that the consultant's "fit for purpose" is usually not properly assessed during the selection process. Defining the specific purpose for engaging a consultant is the key to extracting value from them.

Roles Consultants Can Play

There are many possible reasons for hiring a consultant, and therefore many possible roles that a consultant can play on your next project or initiative. Some of the more common roles and the key issues to be aware of when using consultants in these roles are discussed in this chapter.

TECHNICAL EXPERTISE

The most common reason for organizations to use consultants is to obtain specialized technical expertise that the organization does not generally retain on a permanent basis. This includes such expertise as setting up a business in a new country; contributing technical specifications for a new product; increasing productivity in the call center; or implementing a new human resources system. It is assumed that the consultant has gained this expertise through years of academic education, professional training, management experience within relevant organizations, and the project-based experience of working through similar challenges with many different organizations.

You must carefully assess technical expertise. As discussed in chapters 6, 8, and 9, consulting firms have mastered the art of enhancing their technical credentials. Management and selection teams need to become more streetwise and carefully read between the lines of consultants' technical qualifications, not forgetting that technical expertise often cannot be delivered to the project unless it is supported by other capabilities of the individual consultant or within the consulting firm.

INDEPENDENCE AND OBJECTIVITY

Few, if any, organizations can sustain success through economic cycles or shifting business conditions without having to change—change where they operate, change what they sell, change how they produce, change how they provide service. However, as many organizations do not change very often, over time organization structures become entrenched in the business operating model. Managers' perspectives end up being shaped by the historical mandate of their functional area and the departmental structure through which they obtain and interpret information. The desire to maintain their positions in the organization—which provides them access to information, an ability to influence decisions, and an internal network—and retain control of the resources, budget, and external relationships they currently have drives resistance to any kind of change. This resistance is also influenced by the appetite for risk, which varies by national culture, among other factors (as outlined in appendix 1).

Consultants, as external advisers with exposure to a broad range of experiences and practices, can provide objectivity or an independent perspective uncolored by internal departmental, personal, or political biases. In this way, consultants can introduce a dispassionate array of options driven purely by the needs of the business rather than any vested interest. This independence is also the reason why consultants are often used as facilitators for contentious discussions among management teams.

You must thoroughly understand what motivates the consultant; you cannot afford to assume that they do not have their own agenda and incentives (many of which are discussed in chapters 4 and 5) to recommend one course of action over another.

CONSULTATIVE APPROACH

A consultant's technical expertise or knowledge by itself has very little value if it is not applied in a manner that promotes understanding, acceptance, and application within their client's operation. In many respects, with the ever-increasing depth of content on the Internet, access to information held in proprietary knowledge bases is declining as a differentiator for consultants. Effective utilization and application of that knowledge, however, remains a scarce commodity. Consultants develop their consultative skills through training, project experiences, and coaching. They learn how to read an organization; when and how to ask questions and when to be quiet; to be conscious of all stakeholders who could be impacted by changes; to facilitate workshops; to anticipate areas of resistance in the organization and how to overcome them; and to define communications and to determine to whom, how, and when they should be delivered. This training and experience also allows the consultant to facilitate discussions among parties with opposing perspectives or to broker negotiations to get to a solution that essentially meets the requirements of all the parties. This consultative ability and its value are too often overlooked by buyers of consulting services, particularly on projects that involve extensive changes within the client organization.

You should not assume that every consultant has these consultative skills. All consulting firms and every consultant within each of them do not have the equivalent capability to not only add technical content but also to apply a consultative process to facilitate identification and adoption of solutions that will move the business forward. This capability varies widely depending on the type of consulting firm and the background of the individual consultant. The various types of consulting firms are discussed in more detail in chapter 4.

STRUCTURED PROBLEM-SOLVING APPROACH

By the time managers reach the executive suite, they have a lifetime of experience in solving business problems. They can draw from these experiences to solve new problems effectively and quickly. This is a key strength of mature managers. However, this strength can also be a weakness. Managers may too quickly assume that a solution they implemented in the past will be applicable in their current environment. They may not realize, or take the time to discover, that the context is different and therefore the previous solution is not applicable or transferable. Historically, consultants were trained to devise and apply frameworks and to follow a rigorous, logically structured approach to solving problems thus ensuring that all information is considered and that all possible options are given due consideration when devising a solution to a client problem.

As will be explained in chapter 4, the development of such skills has become less common practice since the mid-1990s. Such capabilities are also underdeveloped within the consulting practices in Asia. Thus, you must ensure that the consultants under consideration have such structured problem-solving capabilities and the ability to apply them on your project.

EXPERIENCE WITH PROJECT METHODS

Consultants are often hired for the process expertise they have gained from executing the same approach or methodology on many different projects. This expertise could include Six Sigma, road maps used for integration of acquisitions, or methodologies to implement an enterprise resource planning (ERP) system such as those marketed by SAP or Oracle. Experienced consultants use methodologies to provide structure and rigor but are also skilled at adapting them to each specific client situation.

The emergence of methodologies is discussed in chapter 4. It is up to you to determine if the consultants really have the actual experience or if they are just planning to follow a methodology that they have not personally used on a previous, similar project. Simply following a methodology will not guarantee the end result; it could in fact waste a lot of time, effort, and money if unnecessary steps are executed or circumstances arise that are not anticipated by the methodology.

PROJECT MANAGEMENT

Project management is different from operational management. In the early stages, projects require a significant amount of detailed planning despite ambiguity and uncertainty regarding tasks and solutions. Interaction among many cross-functional project constituents and stakeholders requires a lot of coordination. All projects have major deliverables and due dates to contend with. Because most executives and managers spend the majority of their time and effort managing day-to-day operations, strong project management skills are not always readily available in-house when required. Because consultants are trained in project management, and project management is integral to each assignment, consultants are often engaged to fill project management roles.

As discussed in chapters 9, 11, and 12, you must verify that the project managers you engage actually have project management experience and that their experience is relevant to the nature of your project.

TEMPORARY RESOURCES

When embarking on a major initiative, particularly one that involves significant application systems development, it frequently does not make business sense to hire additional employees to meet a need that will last only for the duration of the project. Instead, from a cost and human resource management perspective it may be more prudent to contract consultants with the necessary specialized skills to undertake the work and who will depart once the assignment is completed.

When awarding the consulting contract for a team of resources, you, as the buyer, must make sure that every member of the team is qualified—do not simply focus on the few individuals the consulting firm puts the spotlight on. You must also ensure that the consultant team is appropriately configured to transfer knowledge to your own internal resources so that you obtain a lasting benefit. These considerations for vetting and configuring teams are discussed more fully in chapter 4 and chapters 8 through 12 as individual skills and experiences are the core of the capability you are hiring. Don't forget that your intention is for them to be temporary—when the project is completed, you should no longer require them. Chapter 13 covers this topic.

VALIDATE A MANAGEMENT DECISION

Occasionally, management decides on a course of action and then would like to have a respected third party validate or endorse it. Consultants are usually provided the question or problem and asked to come up with an independent answer, often without being given the organization's hypothesis. During the course of the project, internal management may subtly try to influence the consultants so that they come up with the "right" answer. In this way, any fallout from the recommendation—particularly in cases where employee layoffs may be necessary—can be attributed to the consultant rather than management. Or the consultants are simply used to add credence to a significant business decision.

Using consultants in this way may put into question who is actually running the organization. This point is touched on again in chapters 12 and 13.

OPERATE A PART OF THE VALUE CHAIN

Rather than fix or rebuild problematic or inefficient processes, organizations have increasingly outsourced nonstrategic areas of the business to consulting and/or technology firms. These firms contract to deliver specific services with associated service levels for an agreed-upon fee over multiple years.

Although the advantages of the outsourcing model to the consulting industry are significant (as discussed in chapter 4) you should apply considerable thought to your organization's expected benefits from outsourcing and how the value of the contract to your organization can be sustained as market conditions or operating models change from what was envisaged within the contract.

Auditions Needed for Each New Project

On a successful consulting project—one that is well designed and executed and with which your organization's objectives are achieved—consultants may play many of the roles just outlined. In order to obtain returns from your expenditure on consultants, you need to not only clearly define the business problem to be solved but also to understand which type of consulting firm is the most appropriate to help you.

Often, even if managers follow a rigorous process to find a consulting firm that is well suited to address their business problems, they may, based on the consultant's successful performance on the initial project, award the same consultant a new project without getting proposals from other consulting firms. But the new project may require the consultants to operate in a completely different role, perhaps one for which they are not qualified. Rarely will a consultant decline the work, acknowledging they lack the necessary skills or experiences to fill a role. This is especially true if they are the only firm that has been asked to submit a proposal. It is up to you to verify that the consulting firm is qualified to fill the role you wish them to play, because your success in using consultants to deliver measurable value depends on it.

Successful Collaborations

The most successful collaborations we have witnessed between a client and a consulting firm are projects in which specific roles for consultants are precisely defined by the client. These roles included the combination of (a) project management, (b) methodology know-how, (c) technical expertise, (d) consultative approach (particularly for change management support), and (e) resource augmentation for roles that could or would not be staffed internally. Further, the clients were explicit in their expectation that the expert's knowledge would not just be applied to the project tasks but would also be transferred to the client staff. The collective teams were also expected to bring objectivity and to challenge the client's thinking. These were clients who knew how to extract value from consultants.

Case Study 2.1

USING A CONSULTANT IN THE RIGHT ROLES YIELDS POSITIVE RESULTS

A large multinational in a fast-growing emerging market recently assigned a new CEO to their midsize country operation, which had suffered years of underperformance. The CEO, who was new to the region, needed to rapidly gain some independent insight into the market, develop a perspective on the strengths and weaknesses of his management team, and start upgrading the capabilities in his organization. The CEO selected a small consulting firm whose partners would participate directly in the majority of the work and who would leverage assigned client resources, rather than supplying their own team.

Through formal training sessions, open not just to the project team but to the broader organization, the consultants taught company management and analysts about structured problem solving, logical communications skills, and techniques for strategic analysis. The consultants drafted a work plan and sketched out a reporting deck and then directed the client's assigned team members to obtain and capture the necessary data and to create charts and graphs. During workshops the combined team discussed the insights gained from their analysis. The consultants first let the client staff provide their own perspectives and then added their own perspectives and outlined alternative approaches based on their skills and previous experiences. Concurrently, the consultants interviewed all the senior managers (from whom they identified key internal and external issues), formulated suggestions for their resolutions, and identified crippling differences in leadership styles.

Over the course of three months, the consultants were on-site and billable only some of the time, while the client's assigned resources were continually undertaking the tasks for which they were best qualified. During this process the company developed an understanding of its positioning in the market from a consumer, customer, product, and channel perspective; identified the gaps and opportunities to be addressed; and recognized leadership issues that needed to be resolved and developed a plan of action to address them. Because the client's management and employees contributed to much of the work, the company was able to immediately execute against the plan, implementing short-term wins and taking the longer-term steps to establish much-needed competencies. Further, at the end of the project the client had a team of strategy analysts who could and did undertake further analysis without the direction of an external party.

Case study 2.1 illustrates that the CEO clearly understood the roles he wanted his consultant to play:

- Technical expertise related to strategy and leadership development.
- Independence and objectivity, allowing the client's management team and employees to be open and candid regarding the challenges facing the company and permitting a frank assessment of the company's position and management team.
- Consultative approach to facilitate discussion, workshops, teaching sessions in order to promote understanding and move the organization in a new direction.
- Structured problem-solving skills applied to the strategic analysis and developing frameworks to understand the company current and desired positioning.
- Project management capability to devise a work plan, design templates for newly trained employees, provide direction, and report regularly on status.

No Formal Accreditation for Consulting

Finally, you must also understand that the "profession" of consulting has been defined differently by each individual consulting firm. There are no national accreditation bodies as in the accounting, legal, or medical professions that establish minimum industry-defined standards to be met before anyone is able to practice as a consultant. The Certified Management Consultant (CMC) designation is awarded upon application to individual consultants by institutes in certain countries, but most of the major global consulting firms do not mandate accreditation. In many ways, it is advantageous to global consulting firms not to have an industry certification body because without it, buyers are more likely to select known brands that are presumed to maintain quality, rather than to engage certified individuals or consultants from smaller, lesser-known firms. Given the forgoing, you have no guarantee that the consultant you hire—an individual, a boutique firm, or a global firm—will have the necessary capabilities to fill the roles required.

Management Summary

- Many different roles can be filled by consultants. You need to understand the importance of each role relative to the needs of your project.

- Consultants are a valuable management resource when organizations need technical expertise; an independent and objective outlook; a consultative approach to facilitate discussion; a project management capability; or any of the many other roles that a consultant can fill.

- Not all consultants are good at every role. You need to understand the actual capabilities of the prospective consultant relative to the roles to be filled.

- Remember, there is no mandatory accreditation process for consultants.

CHAPTER 3

DEMYSTIFYING THE ECONOMICS OF CONSULTING

DOES YOUR MIND BOGGLE WHEN YOU HEAR OF A BUDGET OF US$50 million for a consulting project, such as implementing a new accounting system for a large organization or designing a global ERP system for a multinational? Do you wonder why using consultants can involve such large project fees?

Racking Up Those Fees

The calculation itself is actually quite simple. The consulting economic model is based on two key levers: the billing rate and the hours worked. Fees are calculated by multiplying the hourly rate for the consultant by the number of hours they spend doing their work. This is the foundation upon which all consulting economic models are built.

The annual revenue generated by the independent or individual consultant is determined by the same two factors:

1. The hourly or daily rate that a client is willing to pay, and

2. The number of hours or days in a year that they are able to bill their clients.

There are upper limits for both of these variables. The rate typically reflects the depth of the consultant's expertise and the availability of such expertise in the marketplace. The rate can vary for a specific consultant depending on the immediacy of the need and the value to the client of the benefit. For example, consultants tend to earn higher rates for due diligence/acquisition work because the window of opportunity for the client is usually short and the value of the overall business transaction is usually high. Consultant fees in this area, despite often being at a premium, are usually no object. The same appears to be true when an organization is in crisis mode!

Standard Rates Are Not That Standard

A common approach used by consulting firms to maximize rates across clients is to publish a standard rate, which is actually their highest rate, and then to discount from the standard rate based on the specific situation in order to arrive at the billing rate. Offering a substantial discount as part of the negotiation process also allows clients to feel that they negotiated a good deal. This approach helps to ensure that the consulting firm does not leave money on the table for clients who would have been willing to pay more or who are poor negotiators.

The Critical Metric of Utilization

There is also a limit to the number of hours a consultant can work since they will eventually be overstretched and the quality of work will deteriorate. In the industry, the annual "standard hours" for a consultant are around two thousand; this total varies by country based on employment regulatory practices, statutory holidays, vacations, and other factors. But not all the time a consultant works is actually billable to a client. Some time is required for marketing, sales calls, proposal writing, project preparation, research, training, travel, internal meetings, etc. Thus, one of the most critical metrics monitored in the consulting profession is utilization—the percentage of a consultant's standard hours that is billed to a client. If all of a consultant's standard hours have been billable then they have been 100 percent utilized. Depending on the type of consulting firm, the majority of good consultants achieve an annual utilization rate of between 80 and 120 percent. Utilization over 100 percent is achieved by working long hours and weekends, which is normal practice.

Maximize Billable Hours

Everyone in the consulting profession is aware that time is money and that any hour not billed to a client represents lost revenue, analogous to an empty passenger seat on a departing airplane. It is accepted that this short-term loss can be justified if that non-billable time is invested in activities that will provide mid-term benefits. These activities, often called "practice development," include marketing, sales calls, proposal writing, developing thought leadership, and training. The biggest waste in the consulting profession is when consultants spend time doing neither client-billable work nor practice development. Not only are these consultants failing to contribute to the short-term or long-term revenue of the firm, they are also not learning or developing new skills.

One technique widely used by consulting firms to minimize wasted hours is to make sure that all consultants, particularly junior consultants, are assigned on a full-time basis to long-term projects. This ensures that a consultant is constantly billing their clients for eight or more hours per day. A long project, of course, minimizes the non-billable gaps between projects. As the client, you may need to assess the need for each resource's time commitment, both from a participation level and a duration perspective. Sometimes, if clients are poor negotiators, this drive to maximize utilization results in consultants billing for the time they spend traveling to or from the client site and on administrative activities such as filling out their expense reimbursement forms.

At the Client's Expense

One final component of the basic economic model is expenses, which can be a material portion of any project's cost. Any expense that is not recovered from a client is a cost to the consulting firm. While most consulting firms are fair in their approach to charging clients for expenses, they sometimes mark up expenses or charge their clients for expenses that are not justified or reasonable (e.g., team dinners just for the consultants, or travel and accommodation for the partner even though he was in town for other reasons as well).

Project Economics

Consulting firms sell projects. Therefore, the primary point at which they measure revenue, and profitability, is at the project level. For any project the actual net project revenue is the sum of the actual revenue across all consultants on the project, less any expenses not recovered from the client (where Σ = sum across all consultants):

$$\textit{Net Project Revenue} =$$
$$\Sigma \textit{ (Billable Hours} \times \textit{Billing Rate)} - \textit{Unrecovered Expenses}$$

Realization is another key metric. It is a proxy for project profitability and is used by many consulting firms. It reflects the percentage of the maximum possible earnings, which is the sum of maximum revenue across all consultants on the project to be actually recovered in the form of revenue for the project.

$$Realization = \frac{Net\ Project\ Revenue}{\sum\ (Standard\ Hours \times Standard\ Rate)}$$

Target realization rates vary by firm and project depending on the standard rate level of the firm, the size of the project, and the attractiveness of the opportunity. Realization of 100 percent would mean that all staff were fully billable at standard rates and that all expenses were recovered. Although most firms do not expect 100 percent realization, the higher the percentage, the more profitable the project. Consulting firms never disclose the realization rate for a particular project, but you can be sure that all internal reviews and approvals will be focused on the realization rate.

Figure 3.1 depicts a simplified costing worksheet for the design and implementation of an ERP system for a single medium-size organization. This type of project has been quite common in the last two decades.

Figure 3.1: Project Costing Example

Factor	Multiplier
Number of Consultants:	12
x Standard Hours:	2,000
x Average Resource Utilization:	90%
x Average Standard Rate:	USD300 per hour
x Percent of Standard Rate:	70%
= **Net Project Revenue:**	**US$4.5 million**
+ Recoverable Expenses:	US$0.5 million
= **Billable to Client:**	**US$5.0 million**
Planned Realization	63%

The example shows that the planned realization, or what the consulting firm hopes to recover, is 63 percent of the maximum possible revenue associated with the standard rates and hours of the consultants on the project.

For this type of project, the initial implementation usually takes about one year and involves a reasonably large team of full-time consultants so that the system can go live at the commencement of the next financial year. Of course, subsequent phases of work to implement additional functionality or to include other corporate entities would increase the total consulting revenue from this typical client. You can only imagine how consulting fees escalate for large organizations and global multicountry initiatives and easily reach the US$50 million level.

If considering such a proposal management must be held accountable for these roles:

- Determining whether deploying so many consultants is indeed the most effective approach to achieve the project objective.

- Validating that there is sufficient value in realizing the business objective to justify the cost.

- Ensuring that the most capable consulting firm has been selected to do the work across all countries or regions within the project scope.

Team Structure Drives Fee Structure

Too often organizations simply accept the project approach and associated fees proposed by consulting firms rather than determining if there are opportunities to change the approach to the work or the structure of the team to minimize consultant head count and/or increase the ratio of internal resources. Management at global corporate offices and government agencies, who typically are working with very large numbers in their normal day-to-day operations, are particularly prone to simply accepting proposals even if they involve significant consulting fees. If presented with a proposal that includes a consulting team or fee that is larger than expected, management needs to take a step back and reassess whether the value to be derived from the consultants justifies the cost and management effort or whether their organization needs to find an alternate approach to meet their objectives.

Management Summary

- Annual revenue for an independent or individual consultant is determined by the consultant's billing rate (standard rate less discount) multiplied by their utilization (percentage of their available standard time that clients will pay for) less any unrecoverable expenses.

- Consultants calculate net project revenue following this formula (where Σ = sum across all consultants):

$$\Sigma \ (Billable\ Hours \times Billing\ Rate) - Unrecovered\ Expenses$$

- Realization, which represents the percentage of possible revenue that is actually earned on a project, is calculated by using this formula (where Σ = sum across all consultants):

$$Realization = \frac{Net\ Project\ Revenue}{\Sigma \ (Standard\ Hours \times Standard\ Rate)}$$

- Consulting firms have the incentive to maximize rates and hours billed to their clients.
  - Standard rates are the consulting firm's highest rate, which they will encourage you to pay. Some discounting may be achieved by those buyers who negotiate.
  - Consulting firms will attempt to assign their consultants full-time for the duration of a long project. You need to determine if the roles such consultants fill necessitate full-time assign-

ment, as well as whether some of the consultants can be rolled off before the end of the project.

- Clients must ensure that the project approach and the mix of internal versus consultant resources make both project and financial sense relative to the organizational objectives to be achieved.

CHAPTER 4

THE CONSULTING PYRAMID SCHEME

ALMOST EVERYONE IS WILLING TO PROVIDE AN OPINION ON SOMEthing. Good advice, however, requires specific expertise, ideally specific firsthand experience, and a reasonably structured approach to identifying and solving the problem at hand. Unfortunately, many advisers provide advice based on subjective opinions absent of any structure, facts, expertise, or relevant experience. Many people are quite willing to express an opinion on something they know nothing about. Charisma and self-confidence, after all, can go a long way.

Single Shingles

Academics, government leaders, and senior business executives have been consulted for generations—they draw upon the expertise and personal experience they have amassed throughout their long careers. Still, today, the most abundant form of consultant is the independent consultant, often referred to as the single-shingle consultant or sole practitioner. Often this individual comes from the academic world or is a retired senior executive of a company or has some specialist technical expertise or was formerly a consultant at a name-brand consulting firm. These independent consultants make money by selling their personal time. Their maximum earnings are constrained by the hourly rate they can charge multiplied by their personal billable hours. Their billable hours are less than their available hours, as they personally have to market themselves and invest time in research/reading/training to remain up-to-date. They also use up time in administration, the extent of which depends on whether they hire an administrative assistant, which would add to their fixed costs. Their greatest challenge while performing billable work is to remain visible in the market so that the gap from the end of one project to the start of the next is not too long.

Few independent consultants can sustain a reasonable level of earnings on a continuous basis because demand for particular expertise commonly goes through peaks and troughs. Thus, it is often preferable to form partnerships to combine client networks, permit greater cross-selling of services, gain some economies of scale to cover overheads, and to normalize revenue levels across multiple partners by pooling income and expenses. While this approach can reduce revenue variability, a cap on individual earnings remains unless clients are willing to pay higher rates or average utilization per individual partner can be increased.

Leverage Increases Partner Profits

To overcome the individual revenue cap, the consulting profession discovered leverage, which next to utilization and realization has become the most significant management metric monitored in the consulting profession. In any project, many tasks—searching the Internet, entering data into spreadsheets, creating charts, and so on—do not require a partner's level of expertise. Consulting partners, those consultants with the most expertise/experience/eminence, can delegate such tasks to less experienced or junior consultants. Clients would be charged a somewhat lower rate for these junior consultants or non-partner resources but that does not mean the total fees will decline proportionately because junior consultants may take many more billable hours than a partner would to perform each task.

The challenge then is for partners to figure out how to leverage themselves across as many junior consultants as possible, and maximize the margin between what is earned from the client for the junior consultants and the compensation costs of those junior consultants. This approach creates a significant revenue boost and an additional key management metric for the consulting economic model:

$$Leverage\ Ratio =$$
$$Average\ Number\ of\ Non\text{-}Partner\ Consultants\ per\ Partner$$

$$Profit\ Contribution =$$
$$Number\ of\ Partners \times Leverage\ Ratio \times Average\ Margin\ on$$
$$Non\text{-}Partner\ Consultants$$

So, what are the implications of leverage for the buyer of consulting services? The upside is that a partner with an expensive billing rate does not perform and charge fees for mundane, low-level tasks. The downside is that the buyer is typically highly influenced by the credentials and sales pitches of the partner(s) and yet, partners are motivated to leverage themselves with less experienced consultants because they generate the margin. Partners will rarely commit themselves full-time to any one project, or even one client, unless the revenue stream (obtained by assigning many junior consultants to the project) more than covers their annual revenue target. Thus, buyers must fully understand what they are actually contracting for in terms of how much time will be applied and what roles will be played by the partners and each consultant on the proposed team and whether that mix makes business sense.

THE ORIGIN OF THE CONSULTING SPECIES

Arthur D. Little, a chemical engineer who studied at MIT, founded what is considered to be the first management consulting firm in 1886 based on a structured, logical, problem-solving approach. Frederick W. Taylor established his consulting practice in 1893 with an emphasis on time and motion "scientific management." Twenty-one years later, Edwin Booz, a graduate of Northwestern University, started his firm. He promoted the concept that companies could be more successful if they could call on someone outside their own organizations for expert, impartial advice. John McKinsey, an accountant from the University of Chicago who is credited with advancing cost accounting disciplines, established his firm in 1926. He formalized what he termed "general surveys" (analysis of companies in financial difficulties) and systemized the process of soliciting new clients, particularly within the financial services community.

These early firms (Arthur D. Little, Booz & Company, and McKinsey & Company remain with us today) were all strongly influenced by academic institutions such as MIT, Northwestern, and Harvard Business School. They also spawned additional firms when partners from these original consulting firms left and started up their own consulting practices.

Each of these firms gave significant thought to how they communicated their findings and recommendations. They produced compelling story lines using a series of logically structured key messages coupled with simple yet content-rich graphics (and, for most of the twentieth century, without the benefit of computers, word processors, or PowerPoint). These consulting firms took pride in the profession of consulting where client interests came first; thought leadership was highly valued; and partners were accountable for developing the next generation of consultants so that they left the firm in better shape than when they themselves had become partner.

After many decades the nature of this profession changed during the 1980s and 1990s with the advent of such projects as ERP systems implementations, process reengineering, and Year 2000 (Y2K) remediation, all of which increasingly relied upon armies of inexperienced junior consultants following predefined methodologies. Given the burgeoning payrolls of a new breed of consulting firm spawned from technology companies, audit firms, and India-based coding shops, it became an imperative to keep selling ever-larger projects to achieve ever-higher revenue objectives. Previously frowned upon brand marketing, sports sponsorships, and overt advertising emerged as key tools to precondition the minds of the executive buyers. As more consulting practices changed from private practices to public companies, revenue rather than client service became the central focus of the major firms in the consulting industry. Advanced telecommunications enabled the ultimate revenue generating model—outsourcing: a model whereby less skilled resources in low-cost locations can be assigned full-time to more repetitive tasks away from the watchful eyes of their clients.

Since the early days of Arthur D. Little, Edwin Booz, and John McKinsey, the consulting industry has been moving away from devising customized approaches to solving problems brought to them by their clients. Instead, consulting firms have increasingly become marketing organizations that package and proactively sell projects on a product-like basis. Reengineering, ERP, Y2K, eBusiness, customer relationship management, outsourcing, and Sarbanes-Oxley have been some of the major waves driving large-scale projects over the past fifteen years. The consulting industry is now looking for the next wave to ride.

The Pyramid Scheme

A partnership can grow revenues from one year to the next by increasing rates, increasing billable hours, and/or increasing the leverage of partners to non-partners. Accordingly, the structure of a consulting firm is designed to maximize the margin on rates, the billable hours (particularly of the least experienced resources), and partner leverage through a pyramid of consultants. A typical example of the structure is depicted in Figure 4.1, which shows a ratio of one partner to twenty non-partner resources.

Figure 4.1: Typical Consulting Pyramid

Title in Firm	Ratio to Partner	Primary Role within Firm	Client Relationship	Role on Projects	Delivery Focus	Compensation
Partner / Principal (12+ years' consulting experience)		Market eminence, sales through client network	Board, CEO, CXOs (CFO, CIO, COO, CMO, etc.)	Provide project mandate Critique output being presented to client	Contracted delivery objectives to client	Share of consulting firm profits
Senior Manager / Director (8–11 years' consulting experience)	2	Manage large projects and internal practice development initiatives	Client executive sponsoring project	Structure project deliverable Provide insights based on findings	Objectives of project sponsor	Salary + meaningful bonus
Manager (4–7 years' consulting experience)	4	Manage small to midsize projects	Managers or department heads	Package slides Preliminary insights	Project deliverables	Salary + bonus
Senior Consultant (MBA or 2–4 years' work experience)	6	Self-directed tasks and / or coordinate sub-teams	Client staff	Creation of raw slide deck	Sub-team analysis	Salary + overtime
Consultant / Associate / Business Analyst (undergraduate)	8	Directed tasks	Client admin staff	Data gathering Data input	Tasks	Salary + overtime

The years of experience shown are indicative only, but nevertheless, they illustrate that historically consultants would have to gain two to four years of project experience at each level before being promoted to the next. Resources have not been developed at the same rate that demand has increased; the result is that competition for experienced consulting resources has intensified. In many cases, the promotion cycle has been accelerated in order to attract or retain talent. This is particularly true in Asia. Beware, consultants may not always have the years of experience that their title would have traditionally suggested. You should not discount the importance of real-world experiences wherein the consultant is continually involved in client projects rather than, as is often the case in start-up/immature practices, simply marketing and proposal writing. The risk to you is that although consultants who have enjoyed accelerated promotion might have the necessary aptitude, they will not have a wealth of experience across multiple projects to apply to your project.

Selling Pyramids, Not People

Given their revenue structure, consulting firms will always want to propose a team that has a mix of consultants across all levels, marrying their practice's pyramid with the goal of getting their junior-level consultants off the bench and billable. It is indeed difficult to obtain an appreciable amount of time from the most experienced consultants on a stand-alone basis. Using a mix of resources from within a consulting firm makes business sense for large projects where there are tasks suited for multiple levels of experience. But if you require only a few highly experienced resources, this will be economically problematic for the consulting firm. Therefore, do not be surprised if your request for a few senior resources yields a proposal for a whole team. Typically, for each more experienced consultant (senior manager or manager) the team will be configured to include at least three less experienced consultants to work under the supervision of that one senior person, who will spend only a portion of their time on your project.

If you are repeatedly asking large or global consulting firms to staff projects with resources from the top end of the pyramid only, they will eventually stop responding to you because staffing in this manner is just not economically viable for them. Once the senior people are assigned to your project, they will not be able to sell projects using only the remaining less experienced people. Therefore, if you require strictly seasoned consultants, you would be better off sourcing them from smaller consulting firms, hiring independent consultants, or hiring permanent staff for these roles.

Some consulting firms try to convince their clients not to worry about the individual resources they assign to a project but to trust in the strength of their global firm. This approach provides the consulting firm with the greatest degree of freedom to assign or reassign resources across multiple clients. Although this greatly benefits the consulting firm, it does not necessarily benefit you as the client.

Time Is Indeed Money

Consultants are typically paid an attractive fixed salary, so consulting firms consider it critical to keep them billable continuously and to extract as much output from them as possible. A few consulting firms use the approach of paying their most junior consultants low salaries but extra for overtime. Generally, however, whether the consultant bills forty or eighty hours a week, their salary is the same, with periodic variable bonuses being directly related to the firm's financial results and the individual's performance. Despite this, the culture of most consulting practices encourages consultants to routinely work sixty to eighty or more hours per week.

There is also a very strong cultural commitment to meet client delivery deadlines. The tendency of partners to be aggressive in their commitments to clients contributes to the need for extended work hours. Consultants in many firms often compete for bragging rights over the number of continuous hours or how many weekends they have worked. Long hours for junior consultants also serve as affirmation that they are important, and are in demand by the most successful partners in the firm. As we saw earlier, one of the performance measures for consultants is utilization, so there is an incentive for consultants to charge as many hours as possible to clients. In our experience, most consultants show integrity when booking hours to clients. It is usually the poorer performers, desperate for billable hours, who may overcharge for services.

Leadership in Thought

In addition to billable hours, consulting firms also place a strong emphasis on continuous learning and developing intellectual capital and thought leadership. This thought leadership further contributes to the development of new consulting frameworks, methodologies, conference presentations, articles, and books. Client engagements provide a wonderful laboratory for the development of thought leadership material and intellectual capital. Consultants are always just one project away from being the expert on any particular topic.

Revenue Targets Drive Behavior

The total value of projects sold—rather than client satisfaction, project profitability, or contribution to thought leadership—has increasingly emerged as the pivotal metric used to assess the value of a partner or senior manager to the consulting firm. Many partners will admit that this is a flawed approach as it can motivate the wrong behavior. The emphasis on sales revenue, for example, drives some partners to attempt to attach themselves, even if their participation is redundant or irrelevant, to the pursuit teams for large projects, with the objective of being able to claim some credit for the eventual sale. This is why you will sometimes have a large team of partners and senior managers presenting proposals to you: not only do they want to guarantee that the project is sold, they also want to be able to claim their piece of the sales action. The main difficulty with sales revenue as a key metric is that the most experienced consultants, the partners and senior managers, are highly motivated to show up during the sales process but are usually not motivated to provide their insight during the engagement or to steer the project away from difficulties.

CONSULTANTS OWE GOVERNMENT A DEBT OF GRATITUDE

It is interesting to look at how U.S. government policy has inadvertently influenced the development and growth of the consulting industry. The first major catalyst was the 1930s' antitrust regulation prohibiting collusion and the sharing of anticompetitive information among bankers, thereby generating the critical mass of corporate investigations and benchmarking work for what are today's well-known strategy boutiques.

Then the 1956 U.S. Department of Justice's antimonopoly decree prohibited IBM from offering professional advice for the installation and use of computers until 1991, creating the opportunity for the large audit firms to build technology and process consultancies.

The Sarbanes-Oxley Act of 2002 caused the consulting industry to undergo mitosis as audit firms spun off their consulting divisions, and then a few years later a new consulting practice emerged within each audit firm. Sarbanes-Oxley likewise created a tidal wave of new work to provide revenue for the audit-based and other consulting firms.

But perhaps nothing has been so beneficial to the growth of the consulting industry as the buying power of government since the public sector typically vies with the financial services sector to be the largest spender on consulting services. During the most recent financial crisis, governments have (inadvertently) helped offset the decline in demand for consulting services in the private sector. Most consultancies now have entire divisions dedicated to the government. This is exemplified by the 2008 Booz consulting separation into the independent businesses of Booz & Company, which targets the private sector globally, while Booz Allen Hamilton focuses exclusively on the U.S. government sector. Government departments usually have a rigorous procurement process to ensure equitable treatment of all suppliers and integrity of the selection process. But given the magnitude of expenditures on consultants by the public sector, is the same rigor applied to ensuring that the necessary value is extracted from the use of such consulting services?

A Variety of Economic Models

The consulting services industry now includes sole practitioners; traditional strategy boutiques; global full-service (strategy, process, systems, and change management) management consulting firms spun-off from accounting entities; newly emerging consulting divisions of the Big Four audit and accounting firms; technology-based consulting units (e.g., IBM, HP); system integrators that were formerly the technology department of large corporations; application consultants of software providers (e.g., SAP, Oracle); Indian-based consulting and outsourcing firms; outsourcing companies; and others.

As depicted in Figure 4.2, the economic models of these various consulting firms differ primarily in terms of which of the variables of rates, leverage, and utilization they emphasize to drive profits depending on their core service areas.

Figure 4.2: Summary of Economic Models of Consulting Firms

Type of Consulting Firm	Consultant Rates	Partner Leverage Ratio	Consultant Utilization
Corporate/Operational Strategy	High	Low	Medium
Process Design	Medium	Medium	Medium
Systems Integration/ Technology Consulting	Low	High	High
Systems and Process Outsourcing	Very Low	Very High	Very High

At one end of the spectrum are firms specializing in business strategy services. They generally need to spend a large portion of their time providing concentrated insights to senior client executives. This necessitates a higher ratio of partner time on each project; this drives down average leverage ratios to only five to eight consultants per partner, which results in a relatively high average hourly rate. System integration firms enjoy leverage ratios of twenty to forty consultants per partner, with a lower average hourly rate because the focus of the work is on applying manpower to build and implement systems using defined methodologies. At the opposite end of the spectrum is outsourcing where contracts guarantee the firm a consistent multiyear stream of work (thus, no non-billable gaps between projects), with leverage exceeding fifty staff.

Creating further complexity in the consulting landscape, the strategy boutiques, in order to expand their revenue stream, have also been broadening their service offerings into process and systems consulting, although the required culture shift and economic model transformation are not insignificant and were not always fully appreciated at the outset. Similarly, firms that originated in the systems and process consulting space have gradually extended their offerings into the other categories of consulting services.

Buyers tend to purchase consulting services based on brand and existing relationships rather than by determining the best fit for the job and greatest value for their money. Because buyers of consulting services have difficulty differentiating between the relative strengths and weaknesses of various consulting firms, these consulting firms have been able to expand their service areas.

Figure 4.3 lists some of the most prominent consulting firms today, showing the service area that we perceive as having been the historical core of the consulting firm, and the additional service areas they appear to have developed strength or capability in. Nevertheless, buyers should be aware that firms will market themselves to be equally capable in all service areas. Consequently, you should look at the economic model of the consulting firm and consider whether the services being offered are appropriate to it from both a capability and a cost perspective.

Global Ambitions Falling Short

The result of this industry evolution is a bewildering array of potential providers of consulting services whose actual capabilities can vary quite dramatically depending on service area and geographic location. Many consulting firms profess to have delivery capabilities around the world. The reality for these global firms is that depth in capable resources exists in North America; capability is strong but sometimes fragmented in Europe (due to the diversity of languages and cultural bias); and capability across Asia ranges from adequate to weak and cyclical. Asia is an emerging market where the consulting firms and the skills of individual consultants are at different stages of maturity, even for global brands. Coupled with the different educational foundations and approaches to skill development in Asia, it makes selection of consultants there highly challenging, a topic that is discussed in more detail in appendix 1.

Figure 4.3: Roots and Capabilities of Prominent Consulting Firms

Company	Consulting Unit Founded	Roots	Corporate Strategy	Operational Strategy	Process Design	Technology/ Systems Integration	Systems & Process Outsourcing
Arthur D. Little	1886	Technology Research			Capable	Core	
Booz & Company	1914	Concept of impartial advice	Strong	Core	Capable		
McKinsey & Company	1926	Budgeting as management tool	Core	Strong	Capable		
AT Kearny	1926/39	Split from McKinsey Chicago office	Capable	Core	Strong		
PA Consulting Group	1943	Worker productivity consultancy		Strong	Core	Capable	
Towers Perrin Consulting	1952	Reinsurance/HR (acquired Cresap McCormick Paget)	Strong	Core	Capable		
Computer Sciences Corp	1959	IT services				Core	Strong
Electronic Data Systems	1962	Outsourcing, servicing GM (now an HP company)				Strong	Core
Steria	1962	Systems development (acquired Xansa)				Core	Strong
Boston Consulting Group	1963	Former Arthur D. Little Partners	Core	Strong	Capable		
Cap Gemini	1967	Data processing (acquired E&Y Consulting)	Core	Strong	Capable	Core	Strong
Roland Berger Strategy	1967	German entrepreneur and government adviser	Core	Strong			
Tata Consultancy	1968	Computer services for Tata Group				Core	Strong
Logica	1969	Systems integration				Core	Strong
Oliver Wyman	1970/84	Integrated with Mercer roots/former Booz Partners	Core	Strong			
Bain Consulting	1973	Former BCG Partners	Core	Strong	Capable		
Fujitsu Consulting	1973	Acquired DMR Consulting				Core	Strong
Atos Origin	1976	IT services				Core	Strong
Infosys	1981	Software services				Core	Strong
Monitor Group	1983	Harvard Business School	Core	Strong			
S&T	1993	Eastern Europe IT distributor for HP		Capable	Capable	Core	
Accenture	2000	Arthur Andersen (1953) then Andersen Consulting (1989)		Capable	Capable	Core	Strong
IBM Global Services	1989	IT services (later acquired PWC Consulting)		Capable	Capable	Core	Strong
Deloitte Consulting	1995/2003	Evolved from audit, later reintegrated into Deloitte audit practices		Capable	Core	Strong	Strong
Bearing Point	1997/2000	European remnants of KPMG consulting post 2009 bankruptcy			Strong	Capable	
E&Y/KPMG/PWC	2004+	Rebuilt consulting capability after post-Enron divestiture			Capable	Capable	
Booz Allen Hamilton	2008	Former US government practice of Booz & Company		Core	Capable	Strong	

Management Summary

- Consulting as a business is a relatively young profession. Its foundation is based on research and a structured approach to problem solving and communications.

- Multiple sole practitioners often form a partnership in order to reduce the variability of income of the individual partners and to share costs.

- Partners of consulting firms are able to expand their aggregate income by leveraging junior consultants and earning the margin on those consultants according to the following formula:

Leverage Ratio =
Average Number of Non-Partner Consultants per Partner

Profit Contribution =
Number of Partners × Leverage Ratio × Average Margin on
Non-Partner Consultants

- You need to ensure that the mix of consulting levels proposed for your project supports the business outcome required, the scale of your project, the roles to be played, and the tasks to be executed.

- Most large consulting firms will resist providing you with only partner/senior manager–level resources without the addition of junior resources that they can leverage. It is just not compatible with their business model.

- The emphasis on sales revenue as an evaluation metric can result in partners being highly visible during the sales process but less so during service delivery.

- Over the past decade, consulting firms have proliferated and the line of services each provides has broadened beyond their original core competencies and economic models making it challenging for organizations to select the appropriate firm.

PART II
SOURCING VALUE FROM CONSULTANTS

CHAPTER 5

YOU, NOT THE CONSULTANTS, NEED TO DEFINE THE PROBLEM

IF YOUR COMPANY IS EXPERIENCING A SLOWDOWN IN GROWTH, A decline in revenue, a reduction in customer volume, or a decrease in profit margins, do you know how you would engage consultants to resolve these issues? The real danger is this: If you do not have a clear perception of the problem, your consultants will undertake to define the problem for you, usually by leaping straight to a solution. This happens because partners in consulting firms have a natural tendency to view your issues through the prism of their own experiences and capabilities. Some may steer their recommended approach toward their own performance objectives, or even the skill sets of their unassigned consultants (recall from chapter 4 that partners are required to get consultants off the bench and billable to clients).

The Problem Is in the Eye of the Beholder

Ask strategy consultants to define the problem, and they may tell you about the need to analyze industry structure and company positioning.

Ask operations consultants, and they may recommend assessing the operational efficiencies of your company. Ask systems integrators, and they will likely suggest upgrading to the latest software, unless of course they have an outsourcing division, in which case every client problem will look like an outsourcing opportunity to them.

Too often business executives deliver a stream of consciousness to the sales-hungry consultant without structuring their thoughts or attempting to formulate their own hypothesis regarding the cause of the issues at hand. Rather, they describe a host of symptoms or provide vague descriptions of the issues of the day and expect that, like magic, the consultants will not only identify the problem but also make the problem go away. The point is that you, as the prospective buyer of consulting services, must separate problems from symptoms and establish the consultants' priorities. Sure, you may need a consultant to aid in the identification of the real problem, but you must be very careful to develop your own perspectives at the same time and challenge the consultants on theirs. If you leave it up to the consultants to define the problem, they will solve the problem as they have defined it, which may not necessarily be the real problem that you need solved. Get this first step wrong and you will generate a stream of consulting work and fees that, in the end, despite much activity, will provide little or no business value.

Case Study 5.1
WHAT IS THE PROBLEM TO BE SOLVED?

After reading numerous articles on the benefits of customer relationship management (CRM), a somewhat autocratic CEO of a leading financial services company instructed his management team to boost their CRM capabilities. Although the CEO believed that his requirements were clear enough, the executives charged with carrying out his instructions were not in agreement regarding the nature of the problem they were being asked to solve. Accordingly, when they solicited CRM proposals from various consulting firms, each firm defined the problem differently. This resulted in a wide range of focus areas and associated recommendations, including:

- Consumer segmentation: Consulting Firm A could identify the market segments to target by leveraging the company's multiyear database created from consumer needs research.

- Customer loyalty: Consulting Firm B could measure customer loyalty by leveraging research and methodologies on customer loyalty and Net Promoter Scores.

- Customer value: Consulting Firm C felt this was the ideal scenario in which to apply their packaged methodology for customer value management and to develop value propositions for the segments of greatest value.

- Call center productivity: Consulting Firm D recommended providing a better customer experience at lower cost via training and process improvements to increase the productivity of the call center.

- Implementing CRM software: Consulting Firm E, associated with a CRM application vendor, discussed the benefits that other clients had obtained from implementing their software.

The company pursued the last option because a technology solution appeared the most tangible. However, after almost a year of presentations, representations, analysis, and deliberation involving the extensive investment of internal management time and staff resources, the company still had very little to show for it. Faced with the steadily eroding patience of the consulting firm, the company wisely disbanded the initiative. This was really a case of a solution looking for a problem, which was why no consensus could be reached on the approach. Luckily, this company did not go ahead and spend the money on the CRM technology solution because shortly thereafter the CEO and his CRM agenda were replaced.

Although perhaps an extreme illustration of the potential impact of unclear problem definition, case study 5.1 is not unusual; such a lack of clarity exists in many organizations when it comes to their projects.

Consultants can be opinionated and persuasive, and they usually come with a take-charge attitude, yet they seldom take ultimate responsibility for ensuring the achievement of the business outcome related to their consulting services. Their primary reasoning, with some justification, is that the client executive is employed to make the management decisions involving the complex intricacies of the business; consultants rarely have access to the kind of information required to make such decisions the way that management does. In addition, consultants have no direct power to influence behavior or to compel action—they rely on the client to do that. Although these are valid points, if the consultants are working on the wrong problem, or the solution is inappropriate, they are irrelevant. So executives and management teams need to consider the broader range of solution options and be willing to challenge the consultants on their definition of the problem, their approach to resolving it, their staffing mix, and their contribution to realizing the required business outcome. It all begins with problem definition.

The Art of Structured Problem Solving

A common and relatively simple technique to define the problem used by many of the strategy consulting firms themselves is drawn from *The Minto Pyramid Principle: Logic in Writing, Thinking and Problem Solving* (1996, Minto International, Inc.) by Barbara Minto, a former McKinsey consultant.

1. Describe the current situation.
2. State what is unsatisfactory about the situation to create the complication that you are now worried about.
3. Define the critical question that needs to be answered in order to resolve the complication—this is the problem that you need to address.
4. Propose a possible answer or your hypothesis of what would solve the problem. Note that there may sometimes be more than one answer to be explored.

The CEO in case study 5.1 could have documented his thoughts more clearly by following *The Minto Pyramid Principle*:

1. Situation: The industry is highly concentrated and saturated, with five competitors accounting for 90 percent of the market. Based on our strong brand and historical success in acquiring new customers we have a relationship with almost 40 percent of consumers in the country.

2. Complication: Our revenue is not growing—our dominant market share, coupled with capable competitors, means that our new customer acquisition rate has been declining and our customer base is contracting.

3. Question: How can we continue to increase our revenue?

4. Answer: Place more emphasis on customer retention and increase revenue per customer rather than simply acquiring new customers.

In this way, he would have clearly articulated the problem and developed a hypothesis for what the potential answer could be. He may have even identified the potential follow-up question—"How do we increase revenue per customer?"—and its hypothetical answer—"Promoting retention, up-selling, and cross-selling within the company's existing customer base." By effectively defining the problem, it would have become very clear to him and his management team what the possible solutions were and what type of proposals should be requested from consultants.

The problem must be stated in the context of the business outcome that is required. In this example, the required outcome was to increase customer retention and revenue per customer. The outcome must be measurable and have a current baseline and a target to be achieved within defined milestone dates. If the problem is not stated in terms of the required business outcomes, then the ensuing projects become focused on the immediate project objective (for example, implement a CRM system), rather than the ultimate business objective.

With the problem more clearly defined, you will be able to specify the type of consultant you require in terms of core competencies and economic model (as discussed in chapter 4) as well as which roles they need to fill (as outlined in chapter 2).

Which Problem to Work On

One additional challenge is determining which problem or set of problems to address first. Unfortunately, problems are never all presented to management at one point in time. Business problems typically arise in random, serial fashion and rarely present themselves in order of severity or with consideration to interdependencies. More often than not business priorities are driven by the agenda or hot buttons of the most politically powerful executives or, at the other extreme, cater to the lowest common denominator and reflect compromises made among the management team. Occasionally, priorities are reordered as a result of whatever a consultant happened to have been pitching to the manager or executive that day. Complicating all this is the fact that executives and managers are typically immersed in day-to-day tactical issues with little time to step back and see the big picture. If they did so, occasionally they would realize that not every problem is of sufficient priority relative to other challenges of the business to justify allocating financial and human resources to its resolution. Therefore, you need to define the priority of the problems you are facing and focus consultants on the high-priority ones, not just the ones they can easily solve.

Unless there is a management framework in place—such as core principles, a well-defined strategic plan outlining the necessary critical capabilities and the gaps that need to be resolved, or an operating model—the sequence in which problems are addressed will be influenced by the subjective considerations of internal management, ad hoc events, and potentially external consultants.

Management Summary

- Do not talk to a consultant until you and your management team have made an attempt to define the problem yourselves; separate symptoms from problems, perhaps using the *The Minto Pyramid Principle*.

- Obtain input from multiple consultants on how they would define the problem. Remember, because your problem will be viewed in the light of their own capabilities you will need to challenge their assumptions and proposed approaches. Try to ascertain if there is some ulterior motive behind the way each of them has defined the problem. Then you, the buyer, must finally determine which consultant has the best understanding of your problem, as well as the most appropriate approach.

- Use an overall management framework to provide an overlay against which to prioritize problems that surface for resolution.

- With the problem defined and prioritized, you should be able to identify the relevant core capabilities required of the consultant, the most appropriate consultant economic model to deliver the solution you require, as well as the role(s) you need the consultant to play.

CHAPTER 6

SEE BEYOND BRAND AND RELATIONSHIP MARKETING

NOW THAT YOU HAVE DEFINED THE PROBLEM, AND HAVE THEREFORE identified the type of consulting capabilities required to undertake the work, you need to investigate which consulting firms have the required capabilities and could potentially take on the problem.

Beware the Brand

It is somewhat of a paradox that the more senior the executive—who should be experienced and perceptive enough to see through the sales strategies—the more susceptible they are to awarding uncontested projects, often of quite substantial scale, based simply on their familiarity with a global brand.

The tendency of buyers to resort to the familiar brand has been a key motivator behind the significant investment in brand advertising that global management consulting firms started to make in the 1990s. It is no coincidence that this advertising investment grew as the head count employed by these consulting firms exploded during that same decade. Advertising became an imperative to ensure a continuous stream of work to keep an ever-burgeoning consulting payroll billable to clients. In the 1980s people used to say, "No one ever got fired for buying IBM." Nowadays, people agree with Adrian Mackay's observation that "No one ever got fired for buying IBM or hiring McKinsey." This is due to the influence that global branding and marketing activities have had on business executives worldwide. After all, it eliminates the inconvenience of vetting the capabilities of a new, unknown consulting firm and convincing management to try an untested service provider.

In the end, despite all the branding and marketing representations about the capabilities of the consulting firm, successful outcomes are almost always determined not by the brand but by the capabilities of the specific individuals working on your project. This is a topic we will come back to throughout this book.

A Relationship Is Not Your Friend

If you have previously engaged a consulting firm in a separate but unrelated area of your organization, they will have established relationships among your management team and will undoubtedly try to use these to convince you that they are the best positioned and most qualified to handle your next project. Their primary argument would be: "Why waste time going through all the effort of identifying and selecting other untested consultants when you already have a trusted relationship with us and we already know your organization?" There is some truth to this statement as the consulting partner—your relationship partner now—will already have some comprehension of your organization's inner workings. But even if you do think that their capabilities may be suited to solving your current problem, it is unlikely that they will be able to deploy the same team again since team members will have moved on to other clients. And even if they are able to provide the same team, your current problem most likely will require different expertise, skills, and roles.

So you still need to go through the process of identifying consulting firms with the capabilities you require, however tempting it is to take the path of least resistance and proceed with a consulting firm you have an existing relationship with. For each engagement you must consider the value-for-money equation and evaluate the consulting firm's depth in your required capabilities relative to what is available in the marketplace. Simply giving the work to the consulting firm that happens to be, or was recently, on-site potentially results in misalignment between problem and consultant capabilities and is a major reason why the value of consulting services delivered to your organization declines over time. As perplexing as it is, it is common for organizations to hire the same consulting firm over and over again even when many in the organization are dissatisfied with the consultant's previous work.

This tendency toward the incumbent is no coincidence. Prior to important project meetings with senior clients many consulting firms role-play the meeting, anticipating questions and objections based on their knowledge of the organization and the individuals they have worked with there. They will develop scripts and practice tag teaming to deliver positioning statements that will appeal to their audience in order to move them toward the consultant's line of reasoning. Most senior executives, on the other hand, will be rushing in from another meeting unaware that the consultants are practically lying in wait for them. Senior executives become entranced by the logically concise, simply illustrated points of view that lead to only one conclusion: award the next engagement to the consulting firm they already know.

Before you know it, what was originally a small US$100,000 project has some time later, without sufficient deliberation or conscious thought, mushroomed across multiple business functions into a multimillion-dollar relationship, with the board demanding an explanation of the business benefits realized from such expenditures. Did all those projects really need to be undertaken, and if so, should they all have gone to one consulting firm? And were they really the best value in terms of capability versus cost? Unfortunately, many companies get caught in this situation.

Cross-Selling—The Easiest Sale

As discussed in chapter 4, consulting firms have different core competencies and different economic models designed to deliver specific types of consulting services. However, consulting firms have a strong imperative to cross-sell a never-ending series of services. Often they start with a service that is a core competence and then cross sell a less mature capability. Cross-selling has a low associated cost of sales. So with the consultant having comparatively easy access to your organization, you—as an existing client—are a prime sales target.

As an example, business strategy firms excel at research, strategic analysis, and applying intellectual rigor to portfolio composition, market positioning, and business model alignment. However, given the nature of their core projects and their cerebrally oriented recruiting criteria, they rarely have staff with the necessary practical experience or aptitude to manage large-scale projects, never mind providing the team for a complex implementation initiative such as merger integration or process and technology implementation projects. Yet corporate strategy firms often extend their services beyond merger candidate identification into activities such as the subsequent operational due diligence and merger integration activities. Similarly, firms whose core strengths are technology consulting are often utilized for business strategy by the client at whose offices they happen to be doing systems work.

Case Study 6.1

RELATIONSHIP MARKETING AND BRAND TRUMP CAPABILITY

The CEO of a U.S. global multinational had been using an eminent global strategy firm for various global corporate strategy projects. On a structural cost-reduction project, one of the recommendations provided by the strategy consultant was to consolidate data centers under one global management company to reduce site costs, to provide better human resource utilization, and to increase purchasing leverage. This sounded like a sensible recommendation. Without considering other firms, the CEO extended the engagement, requesting the same strategy consultants to develop a worldwide data center implementation strategy. As data center operations were not within the core competencies of the strategy consulting firm—they had never actually been involved in moving a data center—their implementation strategy contained only high-level information, and did not recognize the requirements for data center locations nor the extensive planning and preparation that are required to move a data center. Although the recommendations were beautifully documented and packaged, they simply were not viable, and the broader organization would not agree to proceed. A good idea was not implemented because the right consulting firm with the necessary practical expertise was not employed for the design and implementation.

Case study 6.1 illustrates the tendency for organizations to become enamored with their incumbent consulting firms, which usually have an explicit account objective to build the relationships and strengthen the brand image of their firm within the client organization. Consulting partners have the tendency to regard themselves as "masters of the universe"; irrespective of their core competencies, it is natural for them to believe that no client problem is out of bounds for them to solve. It is a slippery slope from the point where a consulting firm is well grounded in their core competencies to where they are way out of their depth in terms of capabilities.

Decentralization Drives Brand-Based Purchasing

According to the Gartner Group's "User Survey Analysis: U.S. Business Consulting: What Customers Want and What Providers Must Do in 2008," for most organizations the decision to buy consulting services is highly decentralized. This means that most organizations do not comprehend the extent of their expenditure on consulting. One of the most telling projects you can undertake is to analyze all of the expenditures within your organization at a country, regional, or global office level. Aside from the insights into operational expenditures, it is not uncommon for executives to be dumbfounded at the amount of money their organization has been spending in the aggregate on consultants. If the analysis is undertaken by one of your incumbent consultants you can watch them squirm as they explain why their firm is on the list of largest vendor relationships by expenditure amount.

Centralized Consultant Selection Advice

Given the decentralized purchasing of consulting services, the fragmentation of selection responsibilities, and the lack of experience among the people responsible for selections, organizations should consider establishing a center of expertise for the procurement of consulting services. This will permit a more dispassionate, independent group within your organization to develop a knowledge base on the various types of consultants in the market and their range of capabilities, to introduce more rigor into consultant selections, and to provide ongoing advisory services to the business sponsor on how to effectively manage consulting contracts.

This procurement function should not simply attempt to extract the lowest price, for as we will discuss in subsequent chapters, the lowest price does not necessarily equate to capability to deliver. Negotiating standardized rate cards with consulting firms is a strategy that some organizations have taken. Yet standard rate cards do not guarantee a reduced price for the overall project—remember, consulting fees are based on billing rates *and* hours worked—unless you can also validate or benchmark the number of hours required for any particular role. Standard rates do not guarantee a standard level of quality either.

The key risk with such procurement functions is that they become bureaucratic, academic, unresponsive, and too far removed from the reality at the field level. They also need to be aware that the capability of consulting firms can vary dramatically across service lines and geographies so that in some locations, or for certain types of projects, other lesser-known niche consulting firms may be more capable of delivering than the well-known global brand.

Finally, a center of expertise for the procurement of consulting services should not be solely focused on making sure that a standard RFP process is followed; they need to make sure business requirements are properly understood and incorporated into the selection decision. Many organizations run a well-defined transparent selection process complete with a hefty RFP, but a closer look reveals that the focus is much more on process (rigor, transparency, and detailed weightings) than content (identification of requirements and insightful assessment of the contending consulting firms), resulting in the selection of a firm for all the wrong reasons (rates, adherence to the process, completeness of response).

Case Study 6.2

GLOBAL OFFICE RELATIONSHIP SPECIFIES CONSULTANT REGARDLESS OF CAPABILITY

An India-based technology firm had undertaken some excellent technology-related work for a senior executive in the global home office of a European multinational. They delivered a successful business outcome by leveraging lower-cost resources, thus also providing excellent value. The consulting partner in the project was able to build a strong relationship with his client executive based on this success. When the India-based technology firm, in their attempt to enter the Japan market, identified an opportunity at the Japanese subsidiary of the same European multinational, the European senior executive at the home office instructed the head of their Japan country unit to use the India-based technology firm. It did not matter that the consulting firm had no presence in Japan, or that the project involved process reengineering, which was not the competency they had applied in Europe. The global senior executive had confidence that the consulting firm would deliver on their commitments because of the importance of the account to the consulting firm. Unfortunately, although the technology firm was familiar with operational processes from a technology perspective, they had no capability to assess an existing process and recommend improvements, nor did they have the language capabilities and knowledge of the relevant business norms and regulations within Japan. The consulting firm quickly lost credibility with personnel in the Japan office and was ultimately replaced. Company time and money were wasted and the Japan-based employees lost all confidence in the firm.

Case study 6.2 illustrates that executives will often project their confidence in a consulting firm to other service areas and geographic regions that they and the consulting firm may be not be familiar with. These executives mistakenly assume that the capabilities of the consulting firm are transferable across services and geographies (the latter in particular rarely being the case, as discussed in appendix 1). Such assumptions and biases simply destroy value for their organizations.

Decision Support Is Available

For certain types of projects, you can purchase comparative reviews to identify consulting firms that may be capable of assisting you. Third-party reviewers or industry analysts such as Forrester Research, Gartner Group, and IDC employ analysts who continually compare consulting firms' services and capabilities. A variety of different frameworks and templates are devised by these firms to help their customers understand who the key consulting firms are and how are they positioned relative to a particular service area. Referencing third-party reviews allows you to broaden your list of consulting firms beyond the familiar brands, your existing relationships, and those that have recently included you in their marketing.

You must be aware that many of these third-party reviews are based on United States–centric data (although a few are extending their geographic coverage) so that ratings may not reflect the consulting firms' capabilities in other regions of the world. For other regions often only head count and revenue statistics are available from analysts, but these are not necessarily a reflection of the capabilities of the consultants within those consulting practices.

Know Your Prospective Consultant

A good way to understand which services a consulting firm is focused on is by browsing through the consulting firm's website. What clients have they served? What service lines do they promote? Where do they have physical offices? What are the profiles of the key partners in the problem areas you wish to solve?

Once a partner or senior manager is assigned to respond to your inquiry, a quick Google search of their name will allow you to determine what industry sectors and topics they are addressing in conference presentations and articles—what they are famous for. If no entries turn up in your search or their reputation is in areas that are unrelated to the problem at hand then this consultant many not be the right one to solve your problem. Publicly available information provides a much better indicator of a prospective consultant's areas of interest and expertise than do their live sales pitches that are tuned to what they think you want to hear.

Discipline Improves Results

You should assess whether (a) project creep, that is, the situation where the same consulting firm continuously undertakes one unrelated project after another, or (b) brand purchasing is an issue within your organization. To mitigate the risks associated with these tendencies, it is a good policy to mandate that a survey of capable firms is undertaken and that a new selection process takes place each time you address a significant new problem involving a new function, process, subject area, or geographic region of the organization. This will ensure that the most capable consultants with the most appropriate economic delivery model are hired to resolve your business problem.

Management Summary

- Branding and relationship marketing have become major tools of global consulting firms in order to recover their huge consulting payrolls from clients.

- Consultants can be sophisticated when it comes to scripting meetings, managing the message, and appealing to your desire for clear, concise propositions or recommended solutions that inevitably lead to the obvious conclusion to hire them—without considering other consulting firms.

- Mandate that any significant new project entailing a different organizational, functional, or geographic scope must result in a new selection process. Do not default to the consulting firm that is currently serving you; the consultants may indeed be capable, but make them prove it in order to secure the best possible outcome.

- Consider establishing a center of expertise for the selection of consulting firms in order to establish more rigor and consistency over the highly decentralized purchasing of consulting services.

- Investigate which type of consulting firm is best equipped to address your current problem from the perspective of its core competency, economic model, roles to be played, and actual local delivery capability; refer to reports from consulting industry analysts.

- Search the Internet to understand how consulting firms and consulting partners are generally presenting themselves; this is a better source of information than their customized sales pitch.

- Assess whether project creep and/or brand purchasing are a problem in your organization.

CHAPTER 7

THE RFP PROCESS: YOUR OPPORTUNITY TO DEFINE THE GAME

A WELL-STRUCTURED REQUEST FOR PROPOSAL (RFP) WILL RESULT in a rigorous and disciplined process to assure that an appropriate consultant (or any vendor for that matter) is selected. Unfortunately, from our experiences on the receiving end of RFPs, it is apparent that too many RFPs are rushed in their development, provide insufficient context in terms of the business challenges, do not emphasize the required business outcome, do not clearly articulate the key requirements, omit a common pricing framework to be followed, and provide too little time for the candidate consultants to respond with a comprehensive proposal. In many respects, the RFP is the most important document in the entire project. If the RFP is not drafted well and contains excessively ambiguous language it is unlikely the appropriate consulting firm will be selected, thus jeopardizing the ability of the project to ultimately produce the required result.

Get Acquainted with Possible Consultants

The best approach to a selection for a project of any scale or significance is to precede the RFP with a request for information (RFI), which achieves multiple objectives:

- Educates you and others within your organization on the problem to be addressed as well as what types of services you can possibly procure from outside your organization.
- Builds interest and commitment from prospective consultants.
- Allows you to consider a broader population of prospective consultants with less time commitment on your part than is necessary for an RFP.
- Includes multiple types of consultants that represent different or mutually exclusive approaches to a project because you will not be doing a rigorous side-by-side comparison (which requires consultants to offer similar services or approaches).
- Provides all possible consultants (including smaller, newer, niche, and obscure firms) a hearing so that you avoid having to include latecomers into the RFP process or explain later why a certain firm was not considered.

Unlike the RFP, the RFI can be a high-level document that provides an outline of your organization, the business problem to be addressed, the list of capabilities you are looking for, the due date for responses to the RFI, the requirements for a formal presentation, and the tentative timeline as to when the RFP will be released. The focus should be on the consulting firm's services and capabilities and you should expect that they will predominately use existing documentation and boilerplates to package a response with limited customization. This allows you to hear about their services without the spin that will get layered on once they more fully understand your requirements. No customized work plan or pricing should be requested; the focus is on understanding their existing capabilities. Do not make the mistake of asking so many questions that your RFI ends up being an RFP in disguise.

You can leverage the information gathered from the various RFI responses to refine your approach to solving your business problem and develop consensus within your organization, as well as to reduce the list to three to five viable candidates. Usually, written responses and presentations from the prospective consulting firms can be useful in educating your internal stakeholders on the art of the possible. The written responses and presentations will also facilitate the start of the internal change process and will, in some cases, help you clarify your vision.

The downside of issuing an RFI is that it requires management time to oversee and it slightly extends the duration of the overall section process, although improving the quality of the process.

At the completion of the RFI response, presentation, and review process, you should officially thank the consulting firms you will not proceed with, at the same time making it clear to them that your decision is final. For those consulting firms that are a possible fit, inform them of the timing for issuing the RFP.

Preparing for an RFP

The objective of the RFP process is to select the most qualified consulting firm available to help you achieve your business objectives at a fair price. The process needs to be well structured and proactively managed, and you should retain the highest integrity throughout. Otherwise, the outcome will lack credibility and you will be subject to unnecessary infighting among different camps in your organization.

CREATE INTEREST AMONG THE CONSULTANTS

Depending on geographic area, stage in the economic cycle, specialization of your needs, and how busy consulting firms are, their level of interest in your project opportunity will vary. You will need to stimulate interest in the project since there is a cost associated with responding to RFPs and the consulting firms may have a limited number of resources available to do so. Some firms may indicate they will participate, but then exert only minimal effort just to maintain the relationship until a more interesting project comes along or internal resources free up. Consulting firms will want to be reassured that you are serious about proceeding with the project and that there is funding for it. They will also want to be assured that no other consulting firm already has the inside track and that they have as good a chance of winning the project as any other firm.

If you are able to generate sufficient interest in your project (the "opportunity" in consulting-speak) the consulting firm will progressively increase the time commitment of a consulting partner in the pursuit, which will fuel their desire to win the work and improve the overall quality of their proposal. If they only have a senior manager pursuing a large opportunity, you can assume they are not fully vested in the opportunity.

CONTROL THE INFORMATION FLOW

Consulting firms will start having internal pursuit meetings where they will map your organization, identifying the key decision maker, the influencers, who they may be able to get to provide inside information and coach them, and who may be a potential roadblock to your selection of them. They will devise approaches to address all these players—even if it means going over your head to more senior executives within your division or up to the global corporate office. Most consulting partners are class acts, professionals who will follow your defined process, counting on their ability to win on the merits of their proposal. But there are some who are adept at managing the sales cycle and who, driven by the size of the project revenue stream, will look for opportunities to secure an unfair advantage.

The sales strategies of consulting firms also may be disruptive to your organization. You need to set the ground rules up front, specifying that all communications must go through a designated point person and that proceeding outside of this framework may result in disqualification. You do not want to give one firm an advantage over others thus allowing them to favorably, but perhaps incorrectly, distort your perception of their capabilities. You do not want to inadvertently end up selecting a consultant who excels at sales tactics over one who can provide the better solution.

One final note on controlling communications: Be sure to have every candidate consulting firm sign a confidentiality agreement at the beginning of the process—even at the RFI stage—because during the process you will undoubtedly have to divulge some proprietary information you do not wish them to share with any of your competitors.

ESTABLISH INTERNAL DISCIPLINE

You will have to communicate internally to those at all levels in your organization who may have an influence on or be impacted by the outcome of your selection.

- RFP Process: Create awareness of the project itself, the RFP timeline, and the names of the consulting firms included so employees are not surprised by the activity.

- Communication Protocol: Advise management and employees that anyone approached by a candidate consulting firm should politely inform the firm that they must get clearance for a meeting by the RFP point person. Some consulting firms, particularly if they are already working within your organization, will find all sorts of pretexts to discuss elements of the RFP with your key personnel.

- Confidentiality: Just as you do not want your information divulged to competitors, consultants do not want their information leaked to their competitors. You should ensure that any verbal or written representations from consultants are not leaked to their competitors by anyone within your organization. Do not share one consulting firm's rates with another or pass on résumés from one consulting firm to another.

- Short List: No one in your organization, other than those in the selection committee, should know who the preferred firm is and who the alternates are. Internal discussions about the consultant should not be mentioned to the consultants in question or their competitors. If the consultants understand their relative competitive positioning you will end up with the least preferred competitors giving up prematurely and the preferred candidates taking the win for granted, which will influence the quality of resources they will commit to staffing your project and their stance on pricing. For example, if a firm believes that they are strongly favored to be selected, they may reduce the strength of their team (so their strong consultants can be placed on other bids or projects) and be less flexible with rate discounts.

Request for Proposal: Your Rules of Engagement

The RFP document must be well written and unambiguous, and it should provide as much information about your company and the project as possible. Appendix 2 provides the table of contents for a typical RFP, although there are many variations depending on the context of the RFP.

PROVIDE THE NECESSARY BACKGROUND DATA

In order for the consultants to define the most appropriate approach, work plan, resource configuration, and pricing, your RFP must contain a reasonable amount of detail. In the absence of detail, the consultant can only make the most conservative of assumptions, which will drive up the number of proposed resources, the timeline to completion, and pricing. In addition, different consulting firms will make different assumptions, thus rendering it impossible for you to compare their proposals on a like-to-like basis. The more detail you can provide, the better the quality of the proposals you receive will be, and the lower the proposed pricing is likely to be.

YOU GET WHAT YOU ASK FOR

A good practice is to provide a table of contents for the proposals that the consultants should follow. This allows you to easily find the information you are looking for in each proposal, particularly if different people on the selection team are responsible for reviewing different aspects of the proposals.

A questionnaire format is another way to standardize the RFP response, or at least part of it. This forces the prospective consulting firms to provide precise answers to your questions. However, creating a spreadsheet and asking them to provide answers in the spreadsheet to hundreds of questions is usually not necessary and can be counterproductive. You are probably never going to be able to digest the response, you will lose sight of the bigger picture, and the responses will be less readable than if they were in a Word document with more readable formatting and in which tables are better supported. Even if you do provide a questionnaire, you should allow the consultants to submit other information that you have not asked for but which they believe is relevant to their proposal.

Wherever you are looking for very specific, detailed information, if at all feasible, prepare templates for consultants to complete, thus making it easier to ensure that all of them provide the same information and that you can easily compare one proposal to another. For instance, it is particularly important that you obtain fee quotations that are broken down in a consistent way (by resource, team, phase, and month). Requesting a summary of all the resources to be assigned to your project is also a good way for you to quickly understand the strength of the proposed team. You may consider providing a template upon which to list resources, with columns for position; level in the consulting firm; number of years of relevant project experience; and list of projects where each key skill or domain area that you require has been involved.

Ideally, you can provide the consultant with your standard contract, asking them to comment on it in their response. If you do not have a standard consulting agreement, have them submit their proposed contractual agreements so that you can evaluate the tone and flexibility of their terms and conditions along with their core proposal. Along these lines, providing your own (either internal or standardized for all consultants) expense policy and requesting confirmation of compliance with it will allow you to manage expectations from the start.

To avoid overly lengthy proposals (it is easier to write a long document than a short one!), consider providing a page limit for each section. This will force the consultants to strip out all the boilerplate text and include solely the information that is relevant for your situation.

DEVELOP THE EVALUATION CRITERIA

To avoid an unstructured, protracted decision-making process after the proposals and presentations have been delivered, devise and document the critical requirements and the relative weighting to be applied to each requirement before proposals are received—preferably even before the RFP is issued. Another benefit of defining the selection criteria while you write the RFP is that you can make sure that you have explicitly requested the information in it that will factor into your decision making.

Some organizations attempt to create intricate spreadsheets with criteria sometimes running into the hundreds. Each individual criterion is weighted and a score on a scale of 1–10 is assigned to each consulting firm for each criterion. This spreadsheet is supposed to produce a magical overall score and ranking for each consultant; the result often defies intuition or explanation, however. At that point people usually start playing around with the weightings and scores to force the spreadsheet to produce the result that the selection team had intuitively arrived at anyway! Of course, this ends up being a recipe for extended discussions, more analysis, and delayed conclusions.

Keep it simple. In this way, there are fewer points for people to contend over. The evaluation criteria for selecting a consulting firm (selecting software is another matter) need not be excessively detailed; otherwise, you will lose sight of the required business outcome. It is necessary for the evaluation criteria to be well structured, documented, and which could look understood by the selection committee.

Criteria can be grouped into those associated with capability to deliver, which might include both products and services and which could look at whether there is value in the firm that can be delivered on the engagement, and those associated with the commercial relationship, which represent the cost and effort associated with extracting the available value. Potential value is therefore a function of these two factors, which can be represented as a formula:

$$Potential\ Value = fn \left(\frac{Capability\ to\ Deliver}{Commercial\ Relationship} \right)$$

We are not suggesting that you try to boil everything down to a number to insert into a formula; rather, we are trying to show that the higher the capability to deliver, the greater the overall cost can be without completely eroding potential value. Obviously, there is a ceiling above which, if costs rise, regardless of the capability, you will not derive value from the consultant.

Applying criteria for capability to deliver will allow you to make sure that there is actually a consulting firm that can do the job, and that you are not simply accepting the best of a bad lot. In fact, by applying this approach, organizations sometimes decide at the end of the RFP process not to hire any consulting firm (regardless of how attractively the work is priced) if none of them has the specific capability that is required to deliver the work.

Occasionally, more than one consulting firm is deemed capable enough to deliver. The differentiating factors to apply in this situation are the criteria related to the commercial relationship. The commercial relationship factors help you determine which consulting firm you will extract value from most successfully.

Figure 7.1 provides some example selection criteria. This list should not be considered exhaustive, and it includes items that may be mutually exclusive, as each criterion depends on the specific role you expect the consultants to play. It is a good idea to publish your criteria in the RFP so that the consulting firms can focus their proposals on the aspects of their offering that matter to you.

Follow a Defined Process

A planned, well-documented process must be established to maintain the confidence of both internal and external constituents and the integrity of the selection.

Figure 7.1: Example Selection Criteria

Capability to Deliver	
Approach	• Does the consultant understand the problem and does their approach to solving it seem reasonable? • Is there a match between the approach (tasks and activities) and the proposed roles (skills and knowledge) for both the consulting firm and the organization? • Is the timeline realistic and acceptable? • Has the consultant convinced you of their capability as a firm to manage such an assignment?
Relevant Experience	• Does the consulting firm as a whole have experience relevant to this project, and will they be able to effectively apply it on the project? • Do they have previous experience working in your industry and country, and in the business function relevant to your project?
Team Composition	• Does the proposed team composition address all skill sets and roles that you identified needed to be filled? • Are the proposed resources the only people capable and available for your project, or is there a larger pool of resources to draw from if additional or substitute resources are required?
Individual Consultants	• Does each proposed consultant have the necessary skills and experience for the role they are supposed to fill? • Are the proposed resources actually available for the project? • Are the proposed resources enthusiastic about the project and any travel or other unique conditions associated with the project?
Ownership and Accountability	• Is the consultant prepared to take ownership of an outcome or result? • Do they see themselves as a determinant of the overall success of the overall project, not just their piece of it?
Knowledge Transfer	• Has the consulting firm proposed a team configuration that will promote knowledge transfer throughout their participation on the project? • Does the consulting firm have a formal approach and plan for knowledge transfer to your resources? • Have they acknowledged the knowledge transfer requirements as a critical component of the project?
Commercial Relationship	
Pricing	• What is the absolute price for the project and how does that compare to your budget and to other proposals? • Is everything included in the price or are you likely to incur lots of additional fees along the way through regular scope changes? • How confident is the consulting firm in their pricing, and are they willing to fix the price?
Contract Terms	• Are their contract terms reasonable? • Do they exhibit flexibility to negotiate mutually agreeable terms?
Partnering	• Have they demonstrated an understanding of your business, project, and requirements? • Is their culture and working style compatible with your management and staff, and with the objectives of the project? • Will they become an integral part of your team? • Are they willing to work with you as a partner rather than strictly according to the terms of a contract?

PROVIDE REASONABLE TIME FOR PROPOSAL PREPARATION

The elapsed time necessary to respond to an RFP is influenced by the size and complexity of the opportunity. The quality of a consulting firm's response will reflect the amount of time you give them to respond. You only penalize yourself if you give consulting firms one week to respond (a favorite practice of Korean companies in particular, to their disadvantage). If the time frame is unreasonably short, and if the RFP is issued at very short notice, the best people of the consulting firm will likely not have the time available to work on the proposal, so the consultants assigned to write the response will be those that are on the bench and who may lack the necessary experience to put together a good proposal.

Allow consultants enough time to truly think through how they will approach your problem; to identify and work through internal processes to secure the right consultants to propose for the project; and to develop a well-structured proposal document. To propose attractive pricing, consultants will need at least a couple of days for their draft proposals to go through risk and pricing assessments within the firm. Otherwise, standard pricing, or standard pricing with a risk premium due to the large number of unknowns usually associated with a short lead time RFP, will be all that they will offer. Therefore, it is good practice to provide all the prospective consulting firms with at least three weeks' notice of a pending RFP release. This will allow the consulting firm to schedule the most appropriate consultants with the necessary expertise to respond to your RFP. If they have participated in an RFI, they should already be well prepared and committed.

Response turnaround times should be in the range of two weeks for a small assignment, four weeks for a large consulting project, and four to eight weeks for a multisite system implementation.

CONFIRM WHO WILL BID

In the RFP you should instruct the consulting firms to email or fax a prescribed form indicating whether they intend to bid, who the primary contact person is on their side, and most important, a commitment that they will comply with your defined process and terms of participation.

This step will confirm for you how many consulting firms will indeed participate, which may be a concern if you are starting with a small set of candidate firms. It also removes any doubt about the communication channels between your point person and their point person.

PROVIDE OPPORTUNITIES FOR CLARIFICATION

Undoubtedly, the prospective consulting firms will have questions after they read the RFP. All questions should be directed to the point person within your organization who can then obtain the requisite answers. As the objective is to secure the best possible proposals from all prospective firms, provided you have informed the firms in advance, you should feel free to share the answers to questions among all firms without divulging where each question originated.

KEEP TO YOUR PLAN

You need to maintain control of the RFP process rather than allow the candidate consulting firms to take control. Consulting partners who perceive themselves to be at a disadvantage relative to others, or who think they have a unique capability that others cannot match, will attempt to shut out their competitors by changing the rules of the game. For example, convincing you to accept a systems-and-process outsourcing proposal as a response to your systems implementation RFP.

Case Study 7.1

UNDERHANDED ATTEMPT TO CHANGE THE GAME

The country operation of a multinational company issued an RFP to two incumbent firms. Firm A believed that they could not secure the business based on merit. In an attempt to gain the advantage, Firm A contacted the immigration authorities and raised concerns about the work visas of a number of the foreign consultants at the project site of Firm B. They hoped to discredit Firm B and prevent key resources from being proposed on the new project. As it turned out, the key resources had valid visas; the raid by immigration officials at the client's project site not only embarrassed client executives but also disrupted the client's project work for a week. Not surprisingly Firm B was awarded the contract.

Case study 7.1 illustrates the lengths that some consulting firms will go to in order to win business, especially when they lack the capability or available resources to win the project fair and square.

PROPOSAL SUBMISSIONS

Proposals should be requested in both hard copy and electronic form. Be sure to ask the consultants to submit sufficient hard copies of their proposals so that you have one for each member of the selection team plus a few extra ones, so you do not have to spend time printing or photocopying before distributing them to the reviewers. Pricing should be submitted in a separate document from the core proposal if you do not want to widely circulate the pricing internally (a practice that promotes confidentiality and reduces bias because of price).

CONSULTING FIRM PRESENTATIONS

Presentations allow the consulting firms to bring their proposals to life and to answer questions you may have. In addition, presentations provide the opportunity for your team to meet most of the members of their proposed team to determine whether there is the right working chemistry. You can observe the dynamics among the consulting team and gauge where the actual expertise lies. You should consider it to be a warning sign if the only person presenting is the partner and the proposed project manager and one or two of the other proposed day-to-day consulting resources are not involved.

Case Study 7.2

A WELL-STRUCTURED RFP PROCESS

While we were employed with global consulting firms, most RFPs we received were substandard documents, and the whole process was poorly managed. But we did have the privilege of being included in a few really well-run selection processes that stand out as examples of companies that defined the selection process to suit the nature of the services being sought to ensure that they truly received the best possible proposals. One of these involved the selection of a consulting firm to undertake a unique, complex, and high-risk project to address issues associated with some out-of-support computer mainframes for which there was a drop-dead completion date. The organization knew there were several different ways to address the problem and different consulting firms would have different approaches as well as tools and resources depending on their particular approach. The company crafted an RFP process that included a full-day session during which very detailed information about the existing technology environment (of course all participants had to sign confidentiality agreements) was provided. Thereafter, the consultants were asked to submit their proposals in three stages. Time was built into each stage for the company to meet with each firm separately to provide feedback on their proposal. Each stage also provided the opportunity for the consultants to withdraw or for the company to eliminate any of the firms.

The first round focused on approach, which allowed the company to identify whether the consultants really understood the problem and had the domain knowledge to define a solution. The next version of the proposal required a detailed project plan and résumés of the resources being proposed. The company was able to assess whether the consulting firms would be able to complete the project within the predefined time period. The third and final version of the RFP focused on pricing, including proposals for penalties or rewards, which was a good mechanism through which the company could see how confident each vendor was in their proposed solution.

The client company had to hire an outside adviser, pay out-of-pocket expenses for the consulting firms who had to fly in experts, take the time to collate the material for the vendors, read and provide feedback on each iteration of the proposal, and answer questions from each vendor. They were able to make a very well-informed decision at the end of the process. What is more, they completed the selection within their planned time frame, thus allowing the project to start as planned and unsuccessful bidders to cut their losses early.

Clearly, the RFP process requires expertise and management time in order for it to be undertaken in a fair and robust manner that will result in the selection of the best consulting firm at an appropriate price to support the realization of your business objectives. Given the impact on your business of failed projects, it is critical to apply the necessary efforts to execute this initial stage competently.

Engaging Consultants to Run the Selection Process

Given what is at stake, you may be tempted to engage a consulting firm to develop the RFP and manage the selection process. There are significant benefits in doing so, as a consulting firm will understand the process, know the potential pitfalls from having been on both sides of the process, and should be able to facilitate a robust contractual relationship with your chosen consultant. But you will need to confirm that the consulting firm has the economic model to resource the selection process cost effectively because a selection process involves periods of concentrated work followed by breaks in activity. You do not want to have to pay for full-time resources throughout the selection process.

More important, you must be extremely careful about conflicts of interests. You will need to confirm with any prospective advisers in the selection process whether they themselves have an interest in responding to the current RFP or a potential follow-on phase. Do they sometimes compete with the candidate consulting firms that you would issue the RFP to? Do they have any financial interests or other relationships with any of the candidate consulting firms or relevant software vendors? Global consulting firms are usually poor candidates to run any type of selection process because their breadth of services means that they have just too many potential conflicts of interest. Typically, you will need to find a boutique firm whose specialist focus or scale of operations prohibits a conflict of interest with either your broader initiative or the candidate consulting firms.

Management Summary

- The best RFPs are preceded by an RFI because they educate your internal organization regarding solution approaches, begin the buy-in process, and allow you to develop a better RFP as well as alert potential consulting firms so that they can adequately prepare to respond to the opportunity.

- To maintain control of an RFI and RFP process, you must proactively explain both internally and externally the protocols for interactions between your personnel and prospective consulting firms. Do not underestimate the potential for external vendor interference or internal politics to derail your process if not managed from the start.

- Develop your evaluation criteria before the RFP is issued to the consultants in order to avoid introducing a bias into your evaluation. Keep it simple in order to remain focused on the required business outcome and reduce the opportunity for protracted analysis and discussion. As potential value is typically made up of both capability to deliver and the overall commercial relationship, it is helpful to categorize criteria into those two dimensions as described in the following formula:

$$Potential\ Value = fn \left(\frac{Capability\ to\ Deliver}{Commercial\ Relationship} \right)$$

- The quality of the proposals you will receive will be a function of (a) the quality of your RFP; (b) the amount of advanced notice you provide the prospective consulting firms; (c) the amount of time you give them to think about and respond to your RFP; and (d) their actual capability.

- The RFP process needs to be well structured and closely managed, and all parties should retain the highest integrity throughout; otherwise, the outcome will not be credible and accepted internally.

- If you decide to engage an external firm to manage the selection process, be sure that no conflicts of interest will bias their approach or prevent candidate consulting firms from participating.

CHAPTER 8

PROPOSALS: THE CONSULTANT'S ATTEMPT TO GAIN THE ADVANTAGE

AS FAR AS A CONSULTING FIRM IS CONCERNED, THE BEST RFP IS THE absence of one. They would prefer a noncompetative situation where they have personal discussions with the prospective or existing client followed by the submission of a two-to-three-page statement of work.

Consultants Are Proposal Writing Machines

Despite their preference not to have to submit a formal proposal, consultants are adept at writing proposals; it is one of their core skills. Proposal writing is one of the first tasks a junior consultant is assigned, and they continue producing proposals at every level throughout their career. By the time they become a senior manager or partner, they are very accomplished at reflecting your perspectives and referencing them in the proposal, positioning their firm, and fashioning a riveting story line that makes you feel compelled to buy their services. You, on the other hand, seldom go through the process of selecting consultants. So who do you really think has the upper hand? The consultant, of course!

Ideally, you should write a formal RFP every time you plan to engage consultants. However, for smaller assignments involving very few consulting resources (although often the initial project is simply the thin end of the wedge for the consulting firm), creating a proper RFP is perhaps too much of a commitment of resources. Be aware of the trade-offs you are making in taking this approach—the time saved on writing an RFP may be spent later on trying to compare potentially very different proposals.

Decoding a Proposal

Effectively evaluating consultants' proposals requires you to decode the consulting terminology and read between the lines to determine what exactly you can expect from the consultant. The following discussion applies whether or not proposals are provided in response to an informal discussion or in response to a more formal RFP.

A common structure for a statement of work or proposal provided by a consulting firm is shown in figure 8.1 followed by an explanation of how to interpret each section of the proposal.

Figure 8.1: Table of Contents for Typical Consultant Proposal

Section 1: Our Understanding of the Situation

Section 2: Our Qualifications to Address Your Problem

Section 3: Scope of Engagement

Section 4: Engagement Approach and Work Plan

Section 5: Our Engagement Team

Section 6: Professional Fees and Expenses

Section 1: Our Understanding of the Situation

Section 1 is the setup. Its purpose is to convince the consulting firm's prospective client that the consultant truly understands the client's situation and proverbially feels their pain. Because consultants usually draw heavily on what you have told them, they are trying to establish a connection or an affinity with you. Their objective is to have you silently nodding your head in affirmation as you read this initial section of the proposal. Naturally, the consultant steers the discussion of the situation toward a definition of a problem that proves most favorable to the capabilities of their consulting firm.

Section 2: Our Qualifications to Address Your Problem

This section is intended to build confidence that the consulting firm can solve your problem. In situations where you are a new prospect to the consulting firm or where their proposed team may have weak credentials, the consulting firm will try to overwhelm you at the beginning of their proposal with the general qualifications of the overall consulting firm. Otherwise, the qualifications may come at the end of the proposal just before or after the fees section to remind you why they are worth it.

Given the way the consulting firm has described the problem, the qualifications provided will conveniently align with your needs by highlighting their experience in situations with similar characteristics. As shown in the example in figure 8.2, they will present an array of logos or a listing of other relevant companies—their clients—for whom purportedly similar projects have been undertaken by the consulting firm. This name-dropping helps to convince you that the consulting firm has been judged capable by organizations similar to yours.

Figure 8.2: Typical Qualifications Page in Consultant Proposal

Our consulting firm's clients include the largest domestic and global banks, insurance companies, and securities firms			
Top 10 Banking Firms (ranked by total assets - 2002)	**Top 10 Securities Firms** (ranked by consolidated capital –2002)	**Top 10 P&C Insurers** (ranked by revenue - 2002)	**Top 10 Life Insurers** (ranked by revenue – 2002)
1. Mizuho Financial Group	1. Merrill Lynch	1. Allianz	1. ING
2. Fin. Tnx Processor# 2	2. Morgan Stanley	2. AIG	2. AXA
3. Sumitomo Mitsui Group	3. Goldman Sachs	3. State Farm	3. Nippon Life
4. National Bank # 1	4. Lehman Brothers	4. Munich Re	4. Aviva
5. Mitsubishi Tokyo Group	5. Salomon Smith Barney	5. Zurich Financial Services	5. Assicurazioni Generali
6. UBS	6. Bear Stearns	6. Berkshire Hathaway	6. Prudential
7. BNP Paribas	7. CSFB	7. Allstate	7. Asahi Life
8. HSBC	8. National Comm. Bank #1	8. Royal/Sun Alliance	8. Sumitomo Life
9. JPMorganChase	9. UBS Warburg	9. Swiss Reinsurance	9. MetLife
10. HypoVereinsbank	10. Charles Schwab	10. Loews	10. Aegon
Source: The Banker	Source: Securities Industry Association	Source: Fortune	Source: Fortune

Our Consulting Firm's Financial Services Industry Clients

What the laundry list of clients being presented also asks you to believe is that the projects undertaken at those organizations are similar to your project *and* that the experiences gained from all those other projects will be magically beamed into the heads of the consultants being proposed for your project. The reality is that unless the proposed consultants have actually worked on those similar projects cited in the qualifications, it can be exceedingly difficult to tap into that experience. Global consulting firms can have thousands of consultants spread around the world, all of whom are busy on their own assignments with very little time or incentive to respond to an email inquiry from a stranger in their firm halfway around the world about how they did things for a previous client. True, most consulting firms have a "global knowledge database," but most client documentation is difficult to decipher and learn from without actually understanding the context of the client project. In addition, previous client work is generally covered by confidentiality agreements and often should not even be shared with other consultants in the firm without first being cleansed, thereby diminishing its value to other consultants and you, the next client!

Given the forgoing, the key questions for you to ask the consulting firm are these:

- "Which clients outlined in the qualifications did the specific members of the consultant's proposed project team work on projects for?"
- "What type of projects were they, and what specific roles did those consultants play during them?"

These questions will help you distinguish between the experiences of the individuals who will actually work on your project and the more tenuous panel of experts and knowledge base that the individual consultants may or may not be able to access during the course of the project.

Section 3: Scope of Engagement

This section of the proposal defines the boundaries of the project, specifically stating inclusions and sometimes exclusions as well. You, as the buyer, have to be very careful that the consulting firm does not define the scope too narrowly relative to your requirements. A favorite tactic with some consulting firms, particularly in competitive situations, is to secure the business through a low-price bid based upon a narrower scope than their competitors'. Subsequently, once the consulting firm has been selected and the project has commenced, they identify multiple areas that are outside of their documented scope for which extra fees will be charged. Considering that you are now committed and inevitably will have tight deadlines, you will have no choice but to approve these change orders.

The proposed scope should be very clearly and tightly defined whether the associated pricing is on a time-and-materials basis (where it is in the consultant's interest for the scope to be as broad and vague as possible) or the pricing is on a fixed-fee basis (where the consultant's interests will be served by defining as clear and precise a scope as possible). More about pricing approaches later in this chapter.

Depending on the type of project, the scope could be defined based on a number of dimensions. An example for an IT-related project is shown in figure 8.3. You need to ensure that the scope of the engagement is defined with sufficient dimensions to provide clarity and to avoid misunderstandings as to the breadth and depth of what is to be achieved. A consultant with integrity will be up front about identifying what is out-of-scope rather than hoping that you simply do not notice what is missing from the in-scope list.

Figure 8.3: Possible Dimensions of Scope (for a System Implementation Project)

Scope Dimension	Description
Business Processes	What is the functional scope of the system from a business perspective?
Level of Automation	Will the system (in the initial implementation or eventually) provide equivalent, more, or less automation than the system it is replacing?
Process Redesign	Should the project critically analyze the business processes and redesign them? Should the new system replicate the existing processes, or, if it is a package, will the organization adopt whatever processes are already embedded in the new system?
Locations	How many locations (and possibly variations of requirements in cases where the locations are in different countries) will be covered?
End Users	Who will be impacted? What different types of staff will use the system? What purpose will the system be used for?
Interfaces	What systems will send or receive data from the new system, and what is the nature of the data and the frequency/timing of these interfaces?
Data Conversion	What level of data will be converted? Balances only or historic transactions and master records? What tolerance will be permitted for reconciliation between the old system and the new system?
Systems to Be Replaced	What existing system and associated functionality must be decommissioned as part of the project?
Reports	What type of reports and how many of each type are required? Will the existing set of reports be reviewed and rationalized first or will they simply be replicated?
Testing Approach	What stages of testing are required in order to accept the system? Will any form of parallel testing will be required? Who will conduct the testing?
Training Approach	What materials need to be prepared and what training must be conducted?

Section 4: Engagement Approach and Work Plan

Consultants are proficient at organizing and structuring work. The multi-phased diagram with high-level descriptors (see figure 8.4) is a favorite way to depict multiple phases in a project. Add some graphical detail and a touch of color, and the path from problem to solution appears to be straightforward. The work plan, usually a Gantt chart, will expand on the phased diagram but will be limited to phase 1, with the level of detail being a clue as to whether the firm in question has actually done a similar project before.

Typically, only phase 1 will be priced. This is to ostensibly limit the financial commitment of the client. But the real purpose of phasing is to mitigate the risk for the consulting firm. They know that before actually starting to work on the first phase they will not fully understand the complexity of the work that will be required in subsequent phases. They will expect to obtain information during the first phase that will allow them to more accurately estimate the level of effort for later phases. The margins for the consulting firm increase with each subsequent phase as they acquire more information and can price work more accurately. If the task descriptions for each phase are at a high enough level, it will also allow the consulting firm to deftly shift some work during the project from one phase to the next phase without the client realizing it and demanding a proportionate reduction in fees. Hence, the need to manage the consultants according to a detailed plan for each phase.

The real advantage of phasing to the consulting firm is that a partner can underprice phase 1 to win the work, knowing full well that once you are committed you have very little option but to continue to utilize them on subsequent phases.

To mitigate the impact of such an approach, at a minimum you should insist that the consulting firm provide "not to exceed" quotations for subsequent phases of work, and you should lock in selected resources and rates for the full duration of the project. Whether consulting firms are willing to submit proposals that lock in fees for future phases depends on you providing as much information as possible to the consultants in the RFP, as well as the level to which the consultant trusts that you are not deliberately withholding information in order to be able to lock in a low fee.

Figure 8.4: Example of Phased Approach

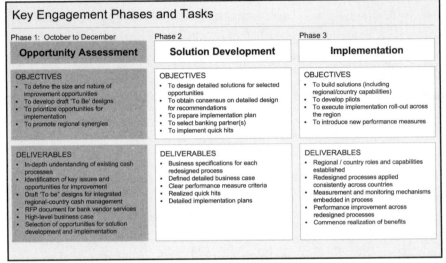

There are other approaches to avoiding being trapped into using the consulting firm that you select for phase 1 for the duration of the project. One is to select two consulting firms for discrete pieces of the work, although this will likely cost you more than if you use one firm exclusively and will require a higher level of management capability to effectively control two competing vendors. Another approach is to issue a new RFP at the end of the first phase, thus forcing the incumbent to do a good job on phase 1 and to provide competitive pricing for phase 2. There are obvious drawbacks to this approach too: a delay between phases 1 and 2; getting other consulting firms to participate, for they will not believe that they have a fair chance; and the amount of information you will have to make available to other consulting firms to level the playing field. And if you do proceed with a new consulting firm, the ensuing loss of knowledge may cause frustration within your organization and could result in key issues or requirements being overlooked.

Section 5: Our Engagement Team

Almost always positioned late in the proposal document, the project team may appear as an afterthought. Up to this stage you are made to believe that the combined worldwide resources of the global consulting firm will be brought to bear on your problem. The reality is that it is the actual members of the proposed project team assigned to the project that will determine its success. However, the experiences and capabilities of the proposed team members are often presented on a generalized high-level basis that at first pass can appear to be impressive—until one starts getting into the details.

Though consulting firms prefer their prospective clients to view the team as a whole package, you need to understand how the team is made up and what the cost implications are. Many consulting firms will not like you asking for more details about each individual consultant because they would prefer that the management and assignment of their resources to be left to their discretion so that they can provide a mix of high-caliber consultants with those consultants who are less capable or experienced. But you should insist on knowing the capabilities of every single team member and then assess if they are the right fit for their proposed role. You are the buyer!

The most important consultant resource in a proposed project team is almost always the full-time project manager (typically a senior manager or manager depending on the scale of the project) as their expertise, day-to-day direction, people management skills, and creativity in overcoming obstacles will determine the quality of the end product. You must be totally satisfied with their capabilities and be convinced that they are fully devoted to your project. To do this, you need to understand what formal project management training they have undertaken, how many projects they have actually managed themselves, the nature and scale of those projects, their perspectives on your project's critical success factors, and the key obstacles to overcome on your project. If the project manager is not presenting an appreciable portion of the proposal presentation, this should be a clear warning sign.

Unless it is a very large-scale initiative, the partner will typically spend ten to twenty percent of their standard time (about five to ten hours per week) on the project providing oversight and insights based on the data collected under the direction of the project manager. Remember from chapter 4, the partner is financially motivated to leverage themselves across multiple projects. Usually, you will have more face time with a partner during the sales process or during pro bono work—which is often the same thing—than at any other point in the engagement. If the partner is the key reason you are hiring the consulting firm, you must determine what will make your project a priority for them relative to their other clients and new opportunities elsewhere.

Project advisers or subject matter experts listed on the project team will be an indication of where the consulting firm feels their team is weak, and where they hope that part-time advisers will be able to offset those weaknesses through cameo appearances. Many project advisers are included in the proposal and sales process but end up participating very little, if at all, on the project. And even if they do actually make their guest appearances, their contribution is often off-key and out-of-sync with the project because they are not specifically focused on your problem; they just relay war stories and anecdotes from their own experience. You must ensure that the consulting firm explicitly states at what points in the project and for what purpose the advisers will be participating.

The actual doers on the project—the senior consultants, consultants, and business analysts—will undertake the majority of the activities, such as data gathering, data entry, data analysis, document creation, presentation development, and providing initial insights on a typical consulting project. To a large extent, they are what your fee payments are covering. Their level of experience will determine how many billable hours they will need to burn to complete a task (taking much less time and therefore less of your money if they have done it before); your staff's perception of the project based on the questions they are asked by these junior consultants; and the quality of the delivered product. The consulting firm will configure teams with a mix of experienced and inexperienced resources at each level even though most firms will bill the client the same rates for all consultants at the same level. This is how the consulting firm deploys its pyramid structure to maximize its leverage of partners to non-partners across multiple projects.

Case study 8.1 shows that you, as the client, do not have to accept the resource mix that is given to you by the consultants. Instead, you can tell the consultants what you would like to see in order to attempt to secure the best value from them.

Case Study 8.1

UNDERSTANDING THE VALUE OF THE RESOURCE MIX

A major U.S. company was undertaking a large-scale project to implement an ERP system across its entire U.S. operations. The project sponsor had previously been a consultant and understood that the value of using a consulting firm for such a project was in the technical expertise required for structuring the project, defining the design components for the ERP system, project management, and facilitating the management of change in the organization. These roles necessitated senior, experienced people: partners, senior managers, or managers. Junior roles for configuring the software could be filled by their own staff (supplemented with lower-cost contractors), who would learn how to effectively design and use the system for future maintenance and enhancements. Accordingly, the company dictated in their RFP that only manager-level or above resources would be accepted in the proposal submission of the consulting firms. The company recognized that this approach would result in a significantly higher average rate per consultant than usual for this type of implementation but believed they would get better overall value for money in terms of system capabilities and benefits to the business. While the consulting firms did not like this structure, the scale of the overall project and the potential for follow-on projects based on relationship selling was attractive enough that a number of consulting firms submitted proposals. The selected consulting firm participated in a project that has subsequently been used as a referenced site within the company's industry sector for the high-value financial benefits that can be derived from an effective ERP implementation.

Case study 8.1 shows that even though consulting firms prefer to have full control over configuring the mix of resources, thus maximizing partner leverage and consultant margin, you do not have to be passive in this regard. It also shows how a greater capability to deliver can offset higher average rates to a company's advantage.

Section 6: Professional Fees and Expenses

Professional fees are always presented near the end of the proposal, as the objective is to first convince you of the consultant's capabilities and the feasibility of their approach so that cost diminishes in importance. You will be reminded that project fees are based on the scope, approach, and resource composition outlined in the proposal.

The approach the consulting firm takes to the pricing will indicate to you where they think the risk is and therefore who they think should bear it for your project.

If they simply provide rates by resource and propose charging you on an hourly-rate basis, it is an indication that they are unable to accurately size the project, perhaps because they do not have the experience they have led you to believe they have. Thus, they are transferring all the risk to you.

If they propose an aggregate, fixed fee then the consulting firm probably has done a similar project before so they are confident that they have a good understanding of the scope and that they can deliver the project within their estimated budget. Or it could be that they don't know much about the project topic, so they are either deliberately undercutting the price to win work in a new area or they simply have no idea what is involved. You will need to figure out their reason to offer a fixed price to avoid getting caught in the difficulties associated with the latter. Regardless, they will put a firm scope management process in place and you will be billed for any variations from their tightly defined scope.

Be aware also that with fixed fees, consulting firms will attempt to hide the specific time commitments for each resource, which provides them with greater resource scheduling flexibility. They will argue that if they are taking the risk they should make the resource decisions. But you would be taking a bigger risk by hiring them without any control over the allocation of resources to deliver your business outcome. You therefore still need to request details on the actual time commitment and when that time will be applied during the project. You should also request the billing rate, inclusive of discounts, for each proposed resource and assess it relative to their qualifications, experience, and role on the project. In some cases, rather than provide an absolute fixed fee, the consulting firm may provide a fee range—for example, from US$250,000 to US$350,000—to allow them some flexibility to deal with unforeseen requirements. However, expect that invoices will magically tally up to the number at the upper end of the range unless you are clear on what the documented assumptions are for the lower versus higher limit.

In most organizations, for budgeting and business case purposes it is necessary to have certainty about what the project will cost. Hourly rates with a cap—a combination of both approaches—is usually the pricing mechanism most client organizations prefer (though consultants do not necessarily like it).

It seems rather one-sided that the consulting firm is guaranteed its fees for simply supplying resources without any downside if the client does not achieve their business objectives. Thus, whenever possible, you should withhold a percentage of the fees until broader project milestones or business objectives are met. This risk-sharing approach will compel the consultant to pay attention to the milestones or objectives that can be attained only as a result of the project, but which are not necessarily achievable within the time frame of the consultant's engagement or which cannot be directly achieved by the consulting firm.

Figure 8.5 summarizes the various approaches to consulting fees; there are many hybrids of these, and they may be used in combination to

Figure 8.5: Fee Approaches

	Hourly Rates	Fixed Fee	Risk Sharing
CLIENT CONSIDERATIONS			
Benefits	Can add or remove resources as needed	Certainty of project costs Consultants will manage change orders	Consultants objectives aligned with clients
Disadvantages	May be difficult to anticipate and control how much will be spent Need effort to carefully manage scope and change orders	No visibility into rates Consultants will be aggressive about identifying change orders Premium paid to the consultant represents value lost to your organization Less control over which resources are assigned Consultants may be inflexible and unreasonably pedantic about what is within their scope	Have to agree on how to determine when fee is payable Will motivate the wrong behavior if the wrong measure is selected
CONSULTING FIRM CONSIDERATIONS			
Benefits	No risk (assuming client does not question value of individual consultants)	Opportunity to earn a premium if hours and expenses are tightly managed	Greater upside potential
Disadvantages	Cannot charge for excess or expensive resources	Risk of overrun	Fees are at risk Client ultimately determines whether to pay
OTHER CONSIDERATIONS			
Best for Projects Where:	Scope is highly unstable or hard to define Resource requirements aren't known at the start The client has primary project management responsibility	The scope is understood and effort is easily estimated by both parties	Tangible, immediate business benefits will be delivered
Variations	Hourly rates with a cap Expenses included	Monthly run rate Expenses excluded	Penalties or bonuses related to deadlines during the project

structure the fee for larger engagements. The best approach will depend on the type of project being considered.

Expenses are usually addressed in a matter-of-fact manner with the assumption being that you will pay whatever invoice is presented to you. Although most client organizations have well-defined expense guidelines for their own personnel, they often allow the consultants they are hiring to get away with extravagances.

Expenses may sometimes be included in a fixed-fee proposal, which will simplify billing for you and the consultant. However, with this approach you will not be able to ensure that expense policies are consistent with yours or to confirm that you are not funding unnecessary expenses.

Read Between the Lines

The forgoing reflects what you should expect in a typical consulting proposal. The contents and sequence are structured to the consulting firm's advantage—designed to convince you that their brand and firm will address your problem. You must learn how to read between the lines and take control by focusing on the capabilities of their individual resources relative to their project role and the feasibility of the approach to the project itself.

As consultants, we wrote our best proposals (and the ones with which we usually ended up winning the business) when we really thought about how we would undertake the project as if we had already won the work. This allowed us to strip out unnecessary boilerplate text, forced us to create very detailed work plans, and compelled us to identify truly capable resources. This took a lot more time than simply responding to the questions posed in the RFP, but it allowed us to develop a high-quality proposal that provided the client with insight into our capabilities. As a client, you must be able to distinguish between proposals that are simply words on a page versus those in which the consultant has already put themselves in your shoes.

Management Summary

- Do not assume that because you are the buyer you have the advantage in the proposal process; you are dealing with people more skilled at writing proposals than you are at assessing them.

- Learn how to decode the proposals to properly evaluate them.

- Consider carefully if the consultant understands your particular situation.

- Drill down on each firm's qualifications, especially where they list previous clients. Have those clients been active within the past three years? Was the work done for them in your functional or geographic area? Which of the cited clients have members of the proposed team actually worked for?

- Be sure the boundaries of the many possible different dimensions of scope are explicitly documented and understood by both parties.

- Be sure to lock in resources and rates and establish "not to exceed" amounts for any future potential phases in a project even if these have not yet been contracted for.

- Focus on the individual consultants assigned to the project, as they will determine the success of your project. Contract to ensure that those resources who were proposed and who you have accepted will actually be the ones assigned to the engagement.

- Decide which approach to pricing you want to engage a consulting firm on the basis of; do not simply accept whatever basis they propose.

CHAPTER 9

SELECTING FOR MERIT AND VALUE

YOU HAVE NOW RECEIVED AND READ ALL THE PROPOSALS, HEARD all of the consulting firms' sales pitches (complete with multimedia slide shows that would make Steven Spielberg proud), and met some members of the proposed teams. The ball is back in your court. The time has come to conduct your evaluation and make a decision about which firm to move forward with so that you can get on with the project.

To Procrastinate Is Not to Decide

Balancing the inclination to spend as much time as you would like to vet all the candidates in sufficient detail versus making a decision with the information that is available at a point in time is a fine art. There will always be more information that you could request from the consulting firms or further analysis you could do on the data available. Many organizations continually defer their selection decision due to their inability to bring the process to conclusion. To them, inaction appears to be safer than making a decision. They often fail to appreciate that protracted inquiry and analysis may undermine the ability to eventually realize expected business outcomes within acceptable time and risk parameters due to the ongoing delay in the start of the project. For example, after management at a U.S. company took an extra two months to evaluate consultants, they finally made a decision and were ready to commence the project. The project was supposed to take ten months, but due to the delay in the selection, the fixed end date was now only eight months away. Management still expected the date to be met without changes in scope, resources, or price. Under pressure, the consultant agreed to the new timeline in order to secure the project, knowing that inevitably quality, scope, price, or a timely delivery would be compromised on what was now a high-risk project.

A good selection process should support management by being well structured, clear on the intent and the process, and transparent to internal stakeholders—and, to a certain extent, to competing consulting firms as well. It should also optimize the effort required to reach a conclusion within a reasonable time frame. This sometimes means that management will be expected to make a selection decision in the absence of complete information.

Occasionally, if your requirements are relatively unique or you are undertaking an initiative or working in a geography where the consulting market is immature, one clear winner—with the necessary capabilities and whose price is right—emerges early on in the process of reviewing proposals and attending consulting firm presentations. Internal consensus under these circumstances is easily achieved. But this situation rarely occurs because the consulting business is crowded with firms that could potentially meet most requirements. More likely you will have to overcome the tyranny of choice and make a decision.

Internal Stakeholder Management

Each consulting firm believes, and will have no hesitation telling you, that they are uniquely capable of meeting your requirements. Not willing to leave anything to chance, especially if there are significant consulting fees at stake, some consulting firms may try to influence the outcome by calling on their existing supporters in your organization who are unrelated to your project but who hold positions of authority. Other consulting firms may try to independently influence and persuade members of your team, the decision makers, and other stakeholders. Approaches can include invitations to expensive meals and tickets to sporting events or other more subtle ones such as offers to run "free" workshops in other areas of the organization and invitations to business conferences. You will need to set internal ground rules regarding communications about the project with the consulting firms, and to police the external candidates throughout the selection process to ensure that the outcome is not bought.

At the same time, your internal stakeholders (without necessarily any prompting by the consulting firms) may already have a preference for which consulting firm they would like to see hired or not hired. Perhaps they were not impressed with the performance of one of the consulting firms on a previous project. Or possibly they are already using one of the candidate consulting firms and they would like to have their choice affirmed by having you select the same one.

Sometimes the bias is more personally motivated. For example, an internal stakeholder may be a former employee of one of the consulting firms or possibly has a friend or close relation who is currently employed by one of the firms. In these cases people may simply promote their favored consulting firm even though they have no understanding of the requirements, alternatives, or facts of the current bid. Only rigorous management of internal stakeholders with constant reminders to them of the project objectives, the selection criteria, and the candidate firms' verified capabilities or shortcomings will ensure that the internal participants are aligned throughout the selection process. This strict attention will also ensure that the decision is made based on the merits of the proposals without being influenced by biases or the consulting firm's direct or covert marketing. In reality, it is rare for everyone to be happy with the outcome of the selection process. You will just have to expect that!

Capability Assessment Activities

Subsequent to the proposals and presentations, further activities may be undertaken to verify capabilities, to assess working styles, or to mold the propositions of the most promising consulting firms more to your needs. These additional activities should have been identified and budgeted during the planning for the selection process. The extent to which you undertake such activities depends on the nature and size of your consulting project. Given this incremental investment of time, you should conduct these additional activities only *after* you have completed your first-level analysis and narrowed down the number of consulting firms to those that are likely to be viable candidates. Use these additional activities to focus on the aspects of the proposals and firms that will allow you to uncover differences among them. The following are examples of additional activities that may help you assess capabilities.

IN-DEPTH WORKSHOP

After reviewing multiple proposals and presentations and obtaining some good ideas from many of them, you should have refined and solidified your own perspective on the best approach to the project, which may not be exactly what any of the candidates have outlined in their proposals. Therefore, it is often beneficial to conduct a detailed workshop with each of the viable firms to understand the rationale for their proposed approach, guide them on your preferences, and identify any weaknesses in their approach as well as determine their ability to mitigate these weaknesses. In the process of doing these workshops, you will be able to assess the reality of their strengths, how flexible they are, whether they can think on their feet, their willingness to adapt and work your suggestions into their approach, and the compatibility of their working style with that of your organization.

This workshop is not a further opportunity for the partner or sales representative to tell you how great their firm is and how committed they are to your organization, or for experts who you will never see again to fly in to impress you. It should be made clear to each consulting firm that this is a roll-up-the-sleeves, working-level session involving the people who will actually be assigned to the project.

RESOURCE INTERVIEWS

If you believe that resources will be a key factor on your project, do not have any reservation about asking to interview proposed individual consultants. It is your responsibility to vet the experience of some or all of the proposed resources in relation to the role they will play on the project. Look beyond the facts presented in a résumé regarding which clients or projects they have worked on and try to understand their actual experience related to each previous project. Sample questions are provided in figure 9.1. The answers to such questions will provide you with a far more accurate impression of their actual capabilities than if they simply describe their previous projects in general. Remember, your confidence in the individual consultants should strongly influence your decision because they will ultimately determine the success of your project.

Also query individual consultants on which specific training courses they have taken. This will give you an indication of their foundation skills and where their expertise and interest actually lie. Ideally, you should be given the opportunity to interview each individual consultant proposed by the consulting firm without the partner, senior manager, or project manager present. For really pivotal resources, it is worthwhile conducting a reference check with one of their previous clients to confirm their role, their capabilities, and the quality of their performance.

Whether the project is going to be charged on an aggregate fixed-fee or an hourly-rates basis should make no difference to the need for you to vet the resources proposed, even though for fixed-fee proposals, consulting firms will tell you that they are taking on all the risk and therefore it is their prerogative to control which resources are assigned to the team. All this effort in identifying your ideal team will have no value, of course, unless the consulting firm contracts to assign these specific resources and agrees that they cannot be withdrawn from the project without your approval.

Figure 9.1: Interview Guideline

Typical questions to ask proposed consulting resources regarding selected projects listed in their résumés

- What were the start and end dates of your participation?
- Was your time commitment part-time or full-time?
- What was your role?
- Who did you report to?
- What were the key activities that you were responsible for?
- What key insights or lessons did you take away from the project?
- What challenges did you experience on the project? How did you deal with them?
- What would you do differently if you were in the same situation again?
- What business benefits did the client realize from the project?
- What lessons would you apply to your proposed project with us?

FOLLOW-UP QUESTIONS

As soon as you have read the written proposals, you will probably have follow-up questions for each of the consulting firms. Perhaps you require clarification on statements in the document or you have identified gaps in the proposal such as a requirement that was not addressed or that was not fully met. While it is usual to cover many of these verbally with the consulting firm during their presentations, interviews, or workshops, it is still a good idea to formally document the questions and require the consulting firms to provide written responses. Such responses are integral to their proposal and would form the basis of the contract should the firm be appointed.

REFERENCE CHECK

Typically, you will have asked for contactable references in your RFP and the consulting firms will have provided a surfeit of these in their proposals. However, turning these into actual, relevant references can sometimes be quite frustrating. Many times consulting firms will not have obtained prior agreement from their references to be cited and interviewed. Or suddenly the referenced company realizes that you are a competitor and they decide they should not be talking to you. You will likely end up being able to contact a very limited number of references so you need to figure out how to get the most out of each reference call. Consider the call to be a one-time opportunity to understand whether the consulting firm and proposed team have the experience that they claim in their proposal.

It is unlikely that dissatisfied customers will be included in the reference list. And you will have no idea about the true nature of the relationship between the reference and the consulting firm. So instead of simply asking whether the client was happy with the consulting firm's work, you will need a strategy for talking to the reference that includes drawing out of them exactly what the consulting firm did and specifically how they contributed to the outcome of the project. This will allow you to determine if the work they are proposing to you is indeed similar to what they have done in the past and to what extent the consulting firm was actually responsible for the success of the previous client's project. If a consulting firm has quoted references in their proposal, but is not able to convert these into people whom you can contact, then you will need to decide how to interpret this in your evaluation.

BAKE-OFF OR PROOF OF CONCEPT

On large, complex information technology implementation initiatives, such as the installation of major new application systems, it can be insightful to have each candidate firm demonstrate their ability to work with the proposed technology. Ask each consulting firm's resources to execute some steps under observation by your selection team, within a constrained time period and using the scenarios you provide them. This will give you a strong sense of how easy they are to work with; the adaptability of their methodologies, approaches, and tool sets; how well versed they are in the technology; and how your system users might respond to them.

Applying Your Criteria

By now your selection criteria will have been defined, focused first on the merit of the proposal or "capability to deliver" and second on overall value or "commercial relationship." You focus initially on evaluating capability to deliver because there is no point in selecting the consulting firm with the lowest price or most flexible partnering arrangements if they do not have the resources or know-how to execute the work. Nor should you eliminate a proposal at this stage because the fees are over your budget.

For each of the criteria, you should be able to build a bullet-point list or comparison table of the significant positive and negative aspects of each of the proposals in order to tease out your overall impression and reach a conclusion.

For example, as shown in figure 9.2, to rate consulting firms on the individual consultants criterion, a side-by-side comparison of the resources proposed in each key role (based on résumés, presentations, or interviews) will help you crystallize your thoughts as to which firm has presented the best collective team and determine any resource-based gaps for projects in which the individual resources are key to success.

Figure 9.2: Example for Evaluation Summary of Individual Consultants

Role	Firm A	Firm B	Firm C	Firm D
Project Manager	✕ Two résumés rejected	✓	★	✓
Team Lead	?	✓	★	✕ Initial candidate failed interview No additional résumés provided
Technical Specialist	✓	★	✓	✕ Résumé rejected No alternate proposed
Overall Team	No	Yes	Yes Plus	No

Legend: ✕ No Suitable Candidate Provided; ? Interview Pending; ✓ Suitable Candidate; ★ Star Candidate

Finding a Capable Consultant

After analyzing the proposals, possibly supplemented by one or more of the capability assessment activities, you should have sufficient information to assess which consulting firms are capable of delivering your project. For purposes of reaching a conclusion and communicating a clear overall picture in your interim updates and final recommendation, it is helpful to summarize any detailed evaluation data into one overall rating per consulting firm for each of the criteria. In figure 9.2, three possible aggregate ratings have been used for the qualifying criteria: "Yes Plus" (exceeds the criterion), "Yes" (meets the criterion), and "No" (doesn't fully meet the criterion). While the evaluation is ongoing, a fourth rating of "Maybe" (additional follow-up steps are required) could be used.

The example in figure 9.3 shows that Firm A has not been able to field the required resources. Though the firm may be capable, they simply do not have the resources available for this engagement. And though Firm D is the incumbent strategy consultant, this type of engagement is not a good fit for them. Only two of the four original candidates are considered to have the capability to deliver and should be further evaluated.

Figure 9.3: Example for Overall Vendor Ratings—Capability to Deliver

	Firm A	Firm B	Firm C	Firm D
Capability to Deliver				
Approach	✓	✓+	✓+	✗
Relevant Experience	✓	✓	✓	✗
Team Composition	✓	✓	✓	✓
Individual Consultants	✗	✓	✓+	✗
Ownership and Accountability	✓	✓	✓	✗
Knowledge Transfer	✗	✓	✓	✓
Overall	No	Yes	Yes Plus	No

Once you have identified the consulting firms capable of successfully executing your project, as a professional courtesy you should inform the firms that have not made the cut so they can release any reserved resources and apply their sales efforts elsewhere. This also reduces your time and effort to manage interactions with multiple competing consulting firms.

When you are communicating with the eliminated consulting firms, you should offer to debrief with them. Debriefing can help you identify ways to improve your selection process for the next time, and it can also help consulting firms improve their offering or their proposal process (it is in your best interest to have many viable consultants in the marketplace). If appropriate you can reassure the consulting firm that they will not be excluded from future opportunities just because they were not successful this time.

Case Study 9.1

NOT EVERY SELECTION RESULTS IN A SELECTION

A multinational company established a new business in an emerging market during the late 1990s and its business grew dramatically over the ensuing years. The rapid expansion of territories, offices, head count, products, and channels spawned convoluted and inefficient operations that threatened to undermine the company's ability to support sales and servicing demands in the years ahead. Consequently, the company created an RFP for process analysis and operations redesign consulting services. It was also a project objective for the consulting firm to transfer some of their process analysis expertise to company personnel assigned to the project. Given the immaturity of the market, there were no local consulting firms with the requisite skills so a number of global consulting firms operating in the country were invited to propose. A short list of three consulting firms submitted their proposals according to the requirements of the RFP.

During the proposal presentations and the subsequent interviews of the project manager and key resources, it became apparent that each of the global consulting firms' proposals drew heavily from proposal materials generated in other countries, with minor customization to address the company's specific situation. Further, none of their proposed staff had worked on the referenced projects that were most relevant to the company's requirements, and few had the necessary process design experience for the company's industry sector. Clearer still was the reality that the local practices of the global consulting firms were still immature, lacking bench strength in process consulting services and the industry sector, although their rates were not in any way discounted to reflect this.

Nevertheless, the company decided that although no firm was deemed capable to deliver, it could leverage the consultative process skills of a consulting firm. Discussions were held with the two most viable consulting firms to see if one of them could provide a project manager, along with a smaller consulting team at a discounted rate to reflect the lack of experience and skills of the consulting firm's proposed resources. One firm responded that they would not undertake any project with aggregate fees less than US$250,000 per month. The other firm declined as well because they could place their resources at full rates at less demanding companies or in positions where the consultant was more qualified.

In the end, the company decided not to proceed with any of the global consulting firms since no firm had the capability to deliver. Instead, although some additional management effort and time were required, the company achieved a more sustainable outcome for this and subsequent projects by building their own internal consulting capabilities—hiring seasoned consultants from the consulting industry, securing subject matter experts on a temporary basis from their company headquarters, and by contracting independent specialists in the market.

Commercial Relationship: Completing the Equation

Now that you have identified consulting firms that are capable of completing the work, it is time to apply further criteria to either confirm your preference if one has emerged as more capable or break the tie if all firms are deemed roughly equivalent in capability. If all firms are equally capable, usually the differentiation will show up in the commercial relationship criteria. These criteria allow you to determine which consulting firm provides the most attractive value proposition, that is, delivery of services for a fair price under mutually acceptable contractual terms and with a commitment to work together to achieve your organization's required outcome. The final decision will in most cases be based on the overall value and synergy that you expect to derive from the relationship over the course of the project. Therefore, you will also need to consider what you are prepared to give up in terms of lower fees and favorable contract terms, if necessary, in order to secure the firm with the best overall capability.

Note that when assessing the commercial relationship, you are primarily evaluating the pricing and terms submitted by the consulting firm as part of their proposal, or in any addendums to it, or pricing submitted in subsequent discussions. So, although you are not entering into any formal price or contract negotiations at this stage, you need to get each consulting firm to submit their best offer. Keep in mind that fees and expenses can often be further negotiated during the contract negotiation stage.

Normalize the Fees

Even if in the RFP you provided a fee template and assumptions that consulting firms should use in their fee calculations, inevitably proposals—and therefore fees—will vary from each other in terms of such items as the size or composition of the team proposed, the duration of the engagement, and the number of working hours per week. You will need to normalize the fees across the proposals by creating a spreadsheet using the approach in figure 9.4 that modifies the fees to eliminate items not required, adds estimates for omitted items, and adjusts for any incorrect or unacceptable assumptions so that you end up with fees that can be compared across consulting firms. You will need a revised fee submission from the consulting firm that reflects the adjustments you believe they should make before you base your decision on these calculations. Your summary will help you identify those adjustments and quickly compare fee proposals across firms.

Similarly, you should create a spreadsheet for the time (measured in hours or days) estimates across the firms to compare individual consultant total costs and rates per hour (or day), and effort per team and phase. Once you complete your analysis it is useful to provide specific feedback or comments to the candidate firms. For example, you may think that one firm's rates are unreasonable for the resources proposed, the assumptions around resource start and end dates are inappropriate, or their overall fee proposal is significantly more than your budget. Raising these questions or voicing these concerns with the consulting firm may result in an immediate adjustment to their proposed pricing or a response that these things can be negotiated if the consulting firm is identified as the preferred consultant. Although this activity is aimed at eliciting their best offer, it should, if at all possible, be limited to a single round of questions and responses. This exchange is often conducted with the consulting firm as soon as you think they are likely to have the capability to deliver; make it clear to the consulting firm, however, that they have not won the work and that their response will simply be considered in your assessment. Your probability of getting fees reduced is higher during this stage, when the firms are still competing, than later, when you have started to negotiate the contract. Contract negotiations are a signal to the firm that they have most likely won, and they will be reluctant to discount their fees at that stage.

Figure 9.4: Example of Fee Normalization Schedule

	Firm A	Firm B	Firm C	Firm D
Base Fee	$5,000,000	$5,500,000	$4,500,000	$3,500,000
Remove Quality Assurance		- $300,000		
Eliminate Contingency		- $225,000		- $350,000
Advance Start Date by Two Weeks	$250,000			
Add Post-Implementation Support			$500,000	
Normalized Fee	$5,250,000	$4,975,000	$5,000,000	$3,150,000

Scrutinize Expenses and Travel Policy

Ideally, you provided a standard expense policy to all consulting firms in your RFP. But in case you did not, or the consulting firms did not agree to them, you will need to evaluate the reasonableness of the projected expenses. In many cases the proposals provide insufficient detail to allow you to do this, so you may need to ask the consulting firms additional questions such as the following:

- Research Documentation: Will you have to pay for research costs (that is, acquiring electronic or hard-copy reports)? If so, who owns such research reports and is there a cap on expenditures above which approvals are required first? This mitigates the chance of consultants purchasing, irrespective of value and cost, research related to your project and then expensing it to you, possibly without even providing you with the original materials.

- Travel Policy: How often will out-of-town consultants return to their home location? Depending on the distance between the project and their home, this might be weekly or less frequently. What impact will these flybacks have on the project? Will they travel during working hours? Will they expect to work some of their billable hours off-site? How will these absences impact your overall project productivity and momentum?

- Travel Costs: What travel class will be used for airlines, hotels, and ground transportation? What per diem rates are expected? Some partners expect to travel first class; many consultants travel business class. Sometimes this is justified, but you should make sure you understand what to expect and are in agreement.

- Incidentals: What are the rates for telephone charges, printing charges, and other incidentals?

- Undefined Expenses: Are there any undefined expenses they are expecting to pass on to you, such as visa fees and incremental business or personal taxes if consultants work outside their home state or country?

- Overhead Allocation: Are they charging you for any overhead expenses: for example, laptop usage, training courses, and administration such as billing activities?

- Expense Margin: Will the consulting firm bill you at cost for expenses or add a margin?

- Internal Expenses: What sort of office accommodation, computers, and other resources will they require on your premises? You may need to incorporate these into your project budget.

You should not hesitate to challenge what seem to be unreasonable or inappropriate expenses, especially any that might be deal breakers, whether it is the absolute amount or the principle involved that you are concerned about. Do not simply accept statements from consulting firms about being required to follow their own internal expense policy. In the end they are spending your money, so if they would like to adhere to their own policies, to retain staff or for other reasons, this should be at their expense. However, at this stage you are simply asking for their best offer and using their proposal and subsequent responses in your evaluation of the firm. Getting final agreement on all the details is usually deferred until formal contract negotiations.

Other Commercial Relationship Criteria

During the review of each candidate consulting firm's proposal, you should examine the contract and identify any terms you think might be problematic or missing. Simply provide each firm with a list of questions and ask for written feedback from them on whether they will agree to vary or include these terms. Do not start to mark up contracts or get into the wording of actual terms at this stage. Again, you don't want any of the consulting firms to assume at this stage that they have won; all you are trying to do is assess whether you will be able to reach agreement on the contract terms, not actually agree to them.

You may have other tie-breaking criteria in the commercial relationship category. The example in figure 9.5 includes a criterion for partnering. Data points associated with a criterion like this are not easily quantifiable, and rating consulting firms will require the selection team to make a subjective assessment based on the interactions with each consulting firm.

Coming to a Conclusion

To come to a conclusion, it is usually necessary to score the candidate consulting firms for each criterion and, possibly using a weighting system, to calculate an overall ranking to identify the consulting firm that offers the best overall commercial relationship. In the example shown in figure 9.5, you can see that because firms A and D were not considered capable to deliver, no further evaluation was made of their proposals other than to review their pricing for benchmarking purposes (as was shown in figure 9.4). For the two remaining consulting firms, analysis of pricing, contract terms, and suitability as a partner yielded a preference for Firm C, even though, as previously illustrated, Firm C's pricing was slightly higher than Firm B's. In certain situations, you may find the difference in capability between two consulting firms is very small, while the difference between them from a commercial relationship perspective is large. In such a situation you may decide to go with the one deemed slightly less capable because their price is significantly lower or because you consider them a more suitable partner.

Figure 9.5: Example for Overall Vendor Ratings—Commercial Relationship

	Firm A	Firm B	Firm C	Firm D
Capable to Deliver	No	Yes	Yes +	No
Commercial Relationship				
Pricing (Fees and Expenses)	-	1	2	-
Contract Terms	-	2	1	-
Partnering	-	2	1	-
Overall Ranking	-	2	1	-

Moving on to Contracting

You should always have at least two candidates—a preferred and an alternate—to move into the contract negotiation stage in order to sustain your negotiating position and to have a backup if contract negotiations with your preferred consulting firm do not go well. For mature consulting markets in North America and Europe, this should not pose any difficulty. In less developed consulting markets, such as those in Asia, it may be more challenging to find multiple capable candidates for certain projects.

Case Study 9.2

KEEP TWO CONSULTING FIRMS IN THE RUNNING UNTIL THE CONTRACT IS SIGNED

The regional office of a major multinational company was selecting a consulting firm for a project that involved designing and implementing a critical application system for the region. After undertaking an RFP process, two consulting firms were identified as having the capability to deliver. On the basis of the superior résumés of the resources proposed, one consulting firm was provisionally established internally, subject to interviewing the proposed resources, as the preferred choice even though they were marginally more expensive than the alternate consulting firm. Contract negotiations commenced, and after much deliberation, the company and the preferred firm were close to agreement on most of the contract terms.

Concurrently, the company conducted due diligence on the proposed resources to ensure that the consulting firm could provide experts to guide and mentor the company's own project team. Over the course of several weeks, proposed resources were interviewed in person or over the telephone. This took much longer than anticipated because several of the resources put forward in the proposal were, in fact, not available for the project, so résumés of suitable substitutes were found and presented by the consulting firm and vetted by the company. Also, interviews revealed that some of the resources were inadequate for the roles for which they were proposed, so the consulting firm had to look for substitutes. After all of the proposed resources had been interviewed, some roles still remained for which there were no suitable candidates.

Knowing at the beginning of the selection process that they were going to spend significant time and effort vetting resources, the company had asked for a commitment that the successfully vetted resources would be reserved for the project, which as outlined in the RFP was scheduled to commence two months later. The preferred consulting firm was unwilling to make the commitment to reserve successfully vetted resources, and indeed some of the vetted resources were withdrawn from the proposed team and assigned to other projects over the subsequent weeks. Regardless of these issues, the consulting firm pushed for the company to proceed with signing the contract, with the promise that appropriate resources would be found for the increasingly long list of open roles. It became apparent that the consulting firm was using the bait-and-switch tactic, and that the proposed or equivalent resources were, in reality, very unlikely to be applied to the project. In addition, the company assumed the risk of being subject to further resource changes initiated by the consulting firm over the course of the project.

The selection team reversed their decision to proceed with what was initially their preferred consulting firm, and instead, the company contracted with the alternate consulting firm, whose resources they had concurrently vetted and who were still reserved. In some cases, the alternate consulting firm offered substitute resources that were superior to those in the original proposal when these resources became available from other projects. The end result was a better overall proposition for the company because the alternate consulting firm also turned out to be more flexible in their contracting approach, agreeing that resources would be changed during the course of the project only with the explicit agreement of the company.

Case study 9.2 illustrates that the selection is not complete (and therefore, the fact that you have selected a preferred candidate should not be communicated to any of the consulting firms) until you have a signed contract—the subject of the next chapter.

Management Summary

- Assess each consulting firm against the criteria you defined when issuing the RFP and develop documentation that supports the scores, rankings, and conclusions.

- Communicate continuously to internal constituents to manage and maintain control of the information flow to consultants as well as to build internal consensus.

- Be alert to attempts by internal constituents to influence your selection based on factors unrelated to the project.

- Focus initially on the attributes that determine capability to deliver rather than getting distracted by pricing and contract terms.

- Undertake capability assessment activities with the viable candidates to confirm your assessments and to allow them opportunities to close any gaps you may have identified.

- Eliminate firms that do not meet the capability to deliver criteria and communicate results to them in a timely manner (unless this would result in only one remaining firm).

- Normalize fees in order to be able to compare them properly and scrutinize expenses carefully.

- Identify your preferred and alternate candidates based on your evaluation.

- Maintain confidentiality regarding your preferences until a contract is signed, since your preferred candidate may change during contract and price negotiations.

CHAPTER 10

CONTRACTING FOR BUSINESS OUTCOMES, NOT JUST LIMITED LIABILITY

FOR MANY ORGANIZATIONS, THE CONVENTIONAL WISDOM IS THAT contracts are best left to the lawyers. However, rather than constructing contracts that reinforce clarity, emphasize commitments, and promote the realization of business benefits, lawyers tend to focus on worst-case scenario issues, such as what will happen if the project fails or if the relationship breaks down. Using marriage as a metaphor for the client-consultant relationship, the contract should be viewed as the marriage vows, which detail what each party is committing to do, rather than a prenuptial agreement, which outlines what happens if the relationship dissolves.

When relationships break down and the parties go to court or arbitration, nobody wins. Regardless of the legal outcome, the company will have failed to realize its business objectives, potentially falling behind competitively in the market. Thus, buyers of consulting services, including whoever is going to be the day-to-day internal project manager, must work with their legal counsel to embed not only the commercial and legal terms, but also the practical project management components within a contract. Rarely, however, do organizations contract with consultants on this basis.

Professional Contracting

Nothing is more frustrating in contract negotiations than when one party includes brand-new requirements after closure has been reached on most of the contract terms. To avoid the delays and confusion this causes, during the first and each subsequent round of negotiations, you should carefully review the contract in its entirety and make all of your required changes to it. You should insist that the consultant do the same. To limit the elapsed time and effort spent on contracting, it is far more effective to make one round of changes each so that you understand the other party's requirements or concerns, and then meet to discuss the terms that you are not in agreement on, than to keep deleting or modifying each other's changes to the contract.

Whose Contract Is It?

Given the extent to which organizations use consultants, it is surprising that more organizations do not have their own standard contracts to provide to all consulting firms. Instead, most consulting firms start with the advantage by issuing their standard contract, which means that all terms are negotiated against wording that is initially biased in the consultant's favor. Any concessions to the buyer are traded off against obtaining more favorable terms to the consultant somewhere else in the contract. It is far better to have your own legal draft, or at least a summary of all the terms that need to be in the contract, to be used as the starting point for negotiation. This does not mean you should not request the consultant's proposed contract as a submission requirement of the RFP. Their contract wording will give you an indication of the terms that may be important to them and where their starting point for negotiation is.

Consulting firms regularly negotiate contracts for consulting services, and typically they even have staff dedicated to this activity. This means they have a significant advantage in this process. If your organization is represented by someone who has negotiated consulting contracts many times and who is knowledgeable about the project, its objectives, and the difficulties it could encounter along the way, then you are much more likely to end up with a fair and reasonable contract.

A Fair Deal

Remember, the contracting process is not about trying to stack the contract with terms that hugely favor your organization, or to attribute all the responsibility for the project to the consultants. A one-sided contract will not generate the teamwork necessary for the project to be successful, nor will it allow you to work through problems jointly. Forcing the consulting firm into a bad position will probably cost you in the long term. Thus, your purchasing function, which may be skilled at driving down the price for physical goods, may not promote the required business objectives because they do not fully understand the impacts to scope and consultant resource selection that arise from squeezing consulting fees. It does not make sense for you to "win" in the negotiation process and then spend the rest of the project chasing the consulting firm to fulfill the onerous and extensive contractual commitments you forced them to agree to. The contract should foster the possibility of a win-win outcome.

Though lawyers sometimes strongly resist this, it is a good idea to include in the contract the actual business objective of the project, the reason for using a consultant, and the rationale for selecting the one that you are actually contracting with. This allows both parties to take a more principle-based approach to resolving issues rather than relying solely on the legal text.

Commercial Terms

At this stage, it is worthwhile to have one final round of discussions about fees to see if there are further reductions that can be applied to the firm's previous best offer. As discussed in chapter 8, there are several ways to define fees for a project, which may include one or more of these categories: hourly rates (with or without a cap), fixed fee, or risk sharing. Regardless of the fee structure, the terms of the contract need to specify the scope of the project so that the client and the consultant are clear on what activities are included in the case of an hourly rates approach, or what the deliverables are for the fixed-fee approach. Financial terms should include rates and a payment schedule.

Any risk-sharing structures need to clearly define the metrics on which the variable compensation is based as well as when they will be measured. While risk-sharing fees are a good way to instill focus on the final outcome rather than on the interim status, they are also the most difficult to specify and to agree on, which means that your contract negotiations will probably take longer.

Case Study 10.1

A BAD CONTRACT CAN DRIVE A PROJECT TO FAILURE

A multinational company was undertaking a multiyear system implementation project in a newly acquired entity in Asia. The local executives of the multinational had flown in advisers from North America to assess what needed to be done to turn around the company. The advisers, who had never worked in Asia and had little appreciation of the country and company culture, recommended a major project to replace all of the existing systems and committed to a time frame and budget based on their experiences in North America. They did recognize the need to hire local experts; however, contracts had to reflect the budget and timeline commitments already made to the company's board. The partner of a local subsidiary of a global management consulting firm, desperate for a sale to meet the current year's revenue target, agreed to a fixed-fee budget and accepted the client's deliberately vague terms of reference without insisting on a clearly defined scope and definitive roles associated with the consulting firm's specific responsibilities, hoping that any difficulties that arose later would be sorted out amicably and fairly between all concerned.

The company also contracted similar ambiguous fixed-fee arrangements with other parties who had substantive roles in the same project. The result was a project with complex interdependencies, significant gaps and overlaps in roles among the parties, and no mechanisms to address unforeseen circumstances given the fixed-fee payment schedule.

It was no surprise that all parties involved with the project squabbled endlessly about scope, roles, and deadlines, and that after multiple delays the project was eventually canceled. All parties ended up in court and the company failed to realize its required business outcome. The original partner had already received his bonus from the "sale," and the consulting firm still retained the fees they had already earned and collected. A new party, the lawyers, also benefited from an unexpected revenue stream. The company, on the other hand, despite the apparently favorably vague and fixed-fee contracts, had made a significant financial outlay without achieving any of its business objectives. It soon sold the operation and withdrew from the market.

Case study 10.1 illustrates not only the negative impacts of ambiguity in expectations, roles, and commitments but also the fallacy of believing that the positive atmosphere during the contracting stage can stand the test of a long, challenging project.

Other Contentious Items

Other than the commercial aspects associated with any project, intellectual property (IP) and confidentiality are often the most fought-over sections of a contract. And seldom do either of these have anything to do with the success of the project itself.

Consultants will invariably insist that they own the rights to the IP contained in the materials produced during their engagement, and at the same time, they will be reluctant to commit to high standards of performance in relation to confidentiality. Wording for these clauses should be negotiated in the light of the project at hand and the fees being paid. As in all contracts there should be recognition of the possible cost or loss associated with adhering to more or less onerous terms. For example, while it makes sense for IP to be owned by whoever can derive value from it, both parties should benefit from the value derived. So, even if you grant the consultant the right to the IP, your organization should also benefit, whether it is through ongoing royalties from earnings by the consultant based on the IP, a onetime payment for the IP, or discounted fees to reflect your contribution to the development of the IP.

Confidentiality is very hard to police; simply dealing with this by describing penalties in the contract may provide you with a false sense of security. The more consultants on the project, the more difficult it is to protect confidentiality. Also recognize that respect for the concept of confidentiality varies by culture. In some countries, company CEOs reluctantly accept that their organization is a proverbial sieve and that once information is released internally, hometown or school or college relationships override any company confidentiality obligations for their staff.

If the project is indeed highly confidential, then the number of individuals privy to such information should be tightly controlled, and the information obtained and deliverables produced must be closely managed. Contracts need to be explicit and state that no materials generated on the project—whether the consultant owns the IP or not—are to be published in the consultant's internal knowledge base or circulated within their firm, and that no client information can be copied from the client-issued computers to the consultant's laptop. And remember that you will likely be held to the same standard of confidentiality you get the consultant to agree to.

It is impractical to impose an indefinite duration on the confidentiality clause, and generally most client information has a fairly limited shelf life. So there is no point in paying a premium for high performance standards in relation to confidentiality if, in fact, this has limited value to your organization. Of course, for information that could damage the organization's reputation or implicate it in any wrongdoing, this is a different matter, although contracts usually explicitly allow consultants to reveal confidential information if it is demanded by a court of law.

Other Must-haves

In addition to the much-agonized-over and much-debated wording concerning IP and confidentiality, a contract should also include the following elements:

- A baseline plan, including detailed definition of deliverables, roles and responsibilities, and the process for agreeing to variations to the plan.

- The identification of key resources, their roles and time commitment to the project, and the procedure for making any resource changes, whether initiated by the consultant or the client. This should also include the process for notifying and agreeing to absences from the project if this would result in a resource spending less than their committed time on the project.

- Your original brief, RFP, or terms of reference, as well as the consultant's various responses to you. Many proposals have wording in the early part of the document disclaiming the consultant's obligation to be bound by what they state in their proposal. What is the point of selecting a firm based on what they have promised in their proposal if they are not prepared to be legally bound by it? The explicit inclusion of such documents, assuming they are sufficiently precise, would greatly reduce ambiguity and ensure that all parties are clear about their commitments.

Contracting need not be onerous if the RFP is well written, the consulting firm's proposal clearly documents the information requested in the proposal, and there is a common understanding of the business objective to be achieved. The contract should reflect what was already offered in the proposal. It is simply ensuring that the consultant is committed to doing what they have said they will do. It is critical that it is precise and complete, as it will become the "constitution" for the project against which rulings on scope, resources, and responsibilities will be made.

Management Summary

- Your internal/external legal counsel can safeguard you against downside risks, but you have to help your legal counsel to assure that the required business outcome is embedded in any contract as the overall objective.

- Contracts should be regarded as "marriage vows," by incorporating the stated business objectives and the structure of the working relationship, rather than as a "prenuptial agreement," which sets out the recourse and liabilities should the relationship not work.

- To start from a strong negotiating position, provide the consultants with your contractual terms or key contract principles instead of using the consulting firm's contract as the starting point.

- Be sure to incorporate the RFP and proposal into the contract to maintain emphasis on the business outcome.

- A baseline plan, which includes scope, responsibilities, milestones, deliverables, and mechanisms for agreeing variances from the plan, is an indispensable part of any contract. Without this information, the rest of the contract is virtually meaningless.

- There is value to intellectual property that consultants should expect to pay for if they wish to reuse materials from your project.

- Be certain you understand the practical limits of confidentiality agreements, particularly in different cultures and countries.

- Do not be taken in by the positive atmosphere prior to project kick-off. In a long, challenging project many things can change. Make sure that the contract explicitly deals with all of the key components that can influence the success of the project.

PART III
SUCCESSFULLY REALIZING THE VALUE

CHAPTER 11

PROJECTS DELIVER VALUE, NOT CONSULTING ENGAGEMENTS

SUCCESS FOR A CONSULTING FIRM IS THE COMPLETION OF A CLI-
ENT engagement, whether the delivery of a report or the implementation
of a new application system. In addition, the engagement would not be
considered successful from the firm's standpoint without the collection
of all outstanding fees and expenses. Even greater success for the consulting firm is securing a follow-on engagement that the consultants can roll
straight onto. This minimizes sales costs and any dip in billable hours
associated with prospecting for a new project elsewhere.

For your organization, however, success is the realization of your
organization's business objectives through the completed project. To
ensure success based on your measures, any engagement with a consulting firm must explicitly state the business objectives to be achieved, the
metrics to be impacted, and the current baselines and targets for each
of the identified metrics. Despite setting these goalposts, it will still be a
constant struggle throughout the project to maintain focus on the business objectives and metrics, rather than the mechanical completion of the
tasks in the project plan, as the definition of success. Simply executing the

project plan does not guarantee that the business objectives will be met. New information or situations always emerge as the project progresses and decisions regarding how to deal with this will have to go back to first principles—the business objective.

The Source of Value

Note the distinction between the concepts "engagement" and "project." Usually, the work a consulting firm contracts for (the engagement) is only a subset of the overall effort required by an organization (the project) for business objectives to be realized. Typically, a consulting firm will complete the engagement before the client realizes the full benefits from the project. Because you, as the manager, will always be ultimately accountable for the project, you would be wise to make sure that the consultant is also rewarded based on the outcome of the project, not simply for the time and effort they have put into the engagement.

To guarantee that the emphasis remains on the business objectives, if at all possible, designate a portion of the consultant's fees as a bonus to be paid only when an agreed-upon set of target metrics are realized. Consultants will argue that they do not have control over all aspects of the client's business, or even the overall project, and therefore they can only be accountable for the engagement itself. However, consultants are usually responsible for defining and structuring the overall project, part of which should be to embed the appropriate actions and changes within the organization to allow the expected benefits to be realized. Therefore, overall project success should indeed be an integral part of their engagement mandate.

If appropriate, particularly if you hold back fees, during the period after the consultants complete their engagement and until you start realizing the benefits, it may be worth having the partner or project manager return periodically to undertake a half-day review of your progress toward realizing the required business benefits. The consulting firm should have a vested interest in you realizing the benefits, regardless of whether fees are at stake, so perhaps you can get their post-engagement review fees waived in exchange for allowing them to use your organization as a reference. For the consultant the advantage is that these return visits give them an opportunity to maintain the relationship and, possibly, to identify other services they can sell you. The point is that many options are available to make sure that the consultant has some skin in the game.

Use Projects to Develop Your People

A secondary benefit of any project should be the improved capabilities of your organization's internal personnel as a result of participating in it. Thus, as many of your qualified people as possible should be embedded in any consulting engagement to provide them with the opportunity to develop their capabilities by working with consultants and observing different approaches to solving business problems. Nevertheless, some consulting firms resist having client personnel included on their engagement team for the following reasons:

- Possibility of exposing weaknesses in their team and work-in-progress deliverables.
- Introduction of uncertainty into the plan because the consultant is not familiar with your staff's work ethic, ability to handle ambiguity, quality of thinking, and attention to detail. Shortcomings in these areas may create additional work for the consulting firm or require additional management time from them.
- Time must be devoted to training and coaching client resources.
- Potential to reduce the number of consulting firm resources required on the project, particularly limiting their opportunity to staff the team with chargeable resources that are effectively no more qualified than your own.

On the other hand, having client personnel on the engagement team can help acquaint the consulting firm with your organization much more quickly and will improve organization buy-in to the project team's recommendations. They can also more quickly find the necessary data and help the project team identify anomalies or inconsistencies in data due to their greater familiarity with the business. Despite some of the initial challenges, the engagement itself and your organization will benefit from the inclusion of your personnel.

There is one caveat, however: you must provide your best and most indispensable resources. When client resources are requested for a project, often the resources that are provided are those that can most easily be spared from their departments. These people are likely to be underperformers, however, and are generally not those who will benefit from working with the consultant or add value to the engagement or project. If you do not provide your best people, the consultants will likely be given incorrect or incomplete information; results or recommendations will be more subject to question by your organization; and the consultants will end up blaming you for any delays or overruns due to the poor quality of resources that you have assigned to "their" team.

In terms of engagement roles, client personnel and consultants usually have different skill sets and competencies given the differences in recruiting criteria, experiences, and normal work environment. However, it is a mistake to allow a consulting firm to execute the engagement solely or predominately with their own personnel. This will undermine your ability to develop your own project capabilities and limit acceptance of the project and its recommendations in your organization. It was common in the twentieth-century consulting engagement model for project teams to consist entirely of consulting staff. Indeed, the conventional wisdom at that time was reflected in a consultants' pricing joke: If we do the project for the client the price is US$1 million, but if we have to do the project with the client, the price is double.

But this attitude should no longer be accepted. The maturity of methodologies, as well as the fact that the skills in using spreadsheets, presentation graphics, and word processing software are no longer the exclusive preserve of the consultant, have made it possible for inexperienced consultants—and therefore also client staff—to participate effectively in consulting engagements. There is no reason why consulting firms cannot provide a training workshop on the techniques they are going to use during the engagement to accelerate your team's acquisition of foundation skills as part of the knowledge transfer process.

Find the Right Mix

Most projects progress through a predictable series of phases. Accordingly, thought should be applied to the appropriate mix of resources from your organization and the consulting firm, which can vary depending on the project nature or phase. And don't forget, sometimes the client resource who may need to participate in project activities may be the executive, the business manager, or the project sponsor.

PROJECT APPROACH AND STRUCTURING THE RESEARCH/WORK PLAN

Defining the approach to the engagement and broader project as well as developing a research or work plan is something consultants do on almost every assignment. You want them to apply their expertise to this stage of your engagement. In fact, the high-level part of this work should already be embedded in their proposal to you. Your challenge, as the buyer, is to get them to broaden their perspective from the engagement scope to the project scope and make sure that this is reflected in the approach. You should also ensure that they have translated their methodology into an actual, resource-based work plan that considers the practical execution aspects in relation to your organization and project.

Though the consultant may lead, you need to do your own thinking, mentally working through the proposed work steps within the context of the business problem being solved; applying your knowledge of your organization; and challenging the consultants, when necessary, about their approach. Make sure that the work plan is not just a regurgitation of their methodology. Question the necessity for each step and how its outcome will be subsequently used on the project. In reviewing the work plan, you should make sure that the impact of your business calendar, local holidays, other projects within your organization, and possible resource contention and availability issues have been identified and reflected in it.

RESEARCH AND DATA GATHERING (INTERVIEWS, SURVEYS, WORKSHOPS)

This is a favorite activity for consulting firms to burn an inordinate number of billable hours, often using consultants with far less experience. Clients rarely raise an eyebrow. It is true that a solid data foundation is necessary to build an accurate fact base whether for competitive analysis, mapping of process activities, or specifying requirements for an application system. Sometimes the independence of a consultant is indeed necessary for client interviews. Due to training and practice, consultants usually have better facilitation skills for leading workshops. However, in most cases, the roles and responsibilities for these activities can and should be shared among personnel of both the consulting firm and your organization to increase the validity of findings, provide a more cost-effective approach, and to improve the capabilities of your resources as a result of doing some of the grunt work. Why pay a premium for basic tasks in which your people can easily participate?

Also, be on the lookout for repetitive work. For instance, if you have ten branches in the scope of the project, do the consultants need to travel to all ten, or can the consultant staff study one as a pilot, fine-tune the approach on a second branch, and then allow your staff, perhaps with some consulting supervision, to study the other eight by focusing on variances in relation to the pilot?

ANALYSIS

This activity represents the activity of highest value the consultants can provide. It is the ability to apply a variety of techniques and bring the expertise of their most experienced consultants to bear against your specific business problem. They will draw heavily on the data that have been gathered, collated, and summarized. Of course, you need to ensure that their most experienced consultants (the partner or senior manager) spend the necessary time contributing to the analysis rather than simply relying on the perspectives of their junior consultants who are gathering the data. Your role is to check the analysis for reasonableness, verify that the conclusions are supported by the data, and challenge the inferences and conclusions.

DOCUMENTATION AND PRESENTATION

Whether the project is oriented to technology (application development or system implementation), process (documenting and modeling process flows), or strategy (creation of financial business models and executive presentations), the activities of this phase can also be shared among the personnel of both the client and the consulting firm. The consulting firm will probably have preferred formats and styles that can improve readability and understanding. Together, the two parties should decide on the required documentation approach, which may include using your own corporate formats and templates rather than the consulting firm's. This will allow you to more easily integrate engagement deliverables with subsequent internal presentations after the consultants depart. This discussion undoubtedly will raise the question as to whether the consulting firm's logo and copyright marks should or should not appear on each page, a subject that optimally should have been addressed during the contracting stage.

CHANGE MANAGEMENT

If done right, the process of making sure that recommendations are accepted, or systems implemented and used, begins at project inception, before any consultants are engaged, and it continues after project completion. Senior executives always underestimate the time and effort required with any initiative that changes internal organization structures, processes, or systems; the result is an underachievement of business objectives. On this point, organizations have only themselves to blame, as adequate attention and effort are crucial to managing change. Someone within your organization, not the consultant, must take responsibility for stakeholder management, communication, buy-in, implementation, adoption, and usage because only those within your organization understand the cultural and political barriers that may impair the realization of the benefits. Consultants can play a strong supporting role by providing advice based on their experiences with similar engagements, imposing more structure and rigor through the use of methodologies tuned to your needs, contributing a more independent perspective, supplying manpower to craft messages, applying specialist implementation expertise, and structuring incentives to promote usage.

Supplement the Team

The key message from the forgoing description of roles and assignments is that you need to determine those areas of the project in which the consultant can provide the greatest value and then supplement the team with your organization's resources. If you leave it up to the consulting firm, they will assign their billable resources to both high- and low-value roles. Case study 11.1 illustrates one example of a project effectively structured to extract the maximum value from consultants.

Case Study 11.1
STRUCTURING A MULTICOUNTRY PROJECT TO BUILD CAPABILITY

A multinational company determined that most of its country operations in a given region were ineffective at the cash management activities of collections, disbursements, and minimizing unnecessary liquidity while maximizing return on float. As each country operation was rather autonomous, a key challenge would be to get them to work cooperatively on a common solution. The regional office engaged a niche consulting firm to provide the necessary level of domain expertise and consultative skills. Two experienced consultants were assigned, and the company provided a project manager from the regional office plus two representatives from each of the five participating country operations.

Together, they covered the accounting, treasury, investments, operations, and information technology functions. The consultants initially participated full-time to orient the project manager; draft the work plan and templates; provide cash management and consulting skills training to the multicountry team; and travel with the team to facilitate the on-site analysis in the first country. After that, on a part-time basis, the consultants coached and remotely supported the client team as they analyzed the subsequent four countries. The consultants then facilitated workshops with the team to consolidate results and agree on the future state vision. They also worked with the team to select a global banking partner to provide cash management services in support of the vision.

Because of the way this project was structured, the multinational company not only realized a massive ROI given the high cash benefit for relatively low external fees, it also developed the skills of eleven of its employees across five countries; broadened their perspectives by exposing them to different cultures and operating practices; secured greater buy-in to the proposed solutions; and accelerated the implementation as the project participants moved on to work with the selected global bank to implement the solution.

Good Things Come in Small Teams

Consulting project scale can be measured on two dimensions: (1) the absolute number of consultants on the project, and (2) the ratio of consultants to client personnel. Generally, the larger the team of consultants the more difficult it is for the organization and business sponsor to extract value from the consulting engagement. First, value lost is a function of the consulting partner's leverage ratio. The higher the leverage ratio, the lower the value that will be added by the most experienced resource in relation to the fees paid.

Second, an increasing number of your personnel will become disenfranchised by the high numbers of external consultants, which in turn creates greater challenges for acceptance of any proposed change. The retort from the consultants will be that your organization is resistant to change. What the consulting firm does not fully appreciate or acknowledge is that the structure of the project—not the objectives nor the work itself, particularly on large-scale projects—is a key contributor to project failure. It is far better to structure projects into smaller, manageable stages with the deployment of a few selected consultants relative to the size of your overall project team. However, most consulting firms would not necessarily suggest such an approach, because it would not get enough consultants off the bench.

Why Pay Extra for Quality?

A number of consulting firms, particularly those undertaking large implementation projects, often assign a partner to assume responsibility for quality assurance. Their time is also charged to the client under the perverse logic that quality is an option that you should pay extra for rather than quality being embedded in the product the firm is delivering and for which you are already paying. In reality, the quality assurance partner is operating in a risk management capacity on behalf of the consulting firm. Their role is to assure that the firm is not exposing themselves to any risk or liability, either in terms of their performance against the contract or in the recommendations they are making. This translates into the reality that the quality of your overall project may or may not be on their agenda. You need to ensure that the role, objectives, and metrics of a quality assurance partner are clearly defined and mutually agreed upon. Do not assume that the presence of a quality assurance partner on the team will guarantee success as you define it.

Extracting Value Takes Management

Finally, it is important to superimpose your objective of extracting value from consultants into the project management process from the start by following some key principles.

PROJECT MANAGEMENT CANNOT BE FULLY OUTSOURCED

The consultant may propose to fill the project management role, which will alleviate the headache of finding your own project manager. This is not recommended. What consulting firms are really providing are not project managers but engagement managers, who are responsible for a subset of the overall project. Who will bring the project to conclusion when the engagement ends if you have not assigned an internal project manager?

Appointing your own project manager, whether as the overall project manager or as a co-project manager working in conjunction with a consulting engagement manager, will not guarantee success, but it will ensure that you have clear line of sight into the project activities and that the communication between the project and your organization is effective. Though consulting firms generally provide very able project managers, this is not enough; knowledge of your own environment in order to anticipate and resolve problems is absolutely key to achieving success.

THE ONLY MEANINGFUL YARDSTICK FOR PROGRESS IS THE PLAN

To get an accurate assessment of the status of the project you need to be sure that there is a well-thought-out, detailed plan tying resources into activities, deliverables, and deadlines. In addition, there should be a practical way of assessing what progress has been made each week against the plan at a detailed level. If the consultant is not doing this it indicates that your project is not being well managed by the consultants.

ISSUES ALWAYS DELAY THE PROJECT, BUT THEY SHOULD NOT NECESSARILY IMPACT FEES

Implement a robust process for managing risks because once they materialize into actual events they will almost certainly delay your project. It is at this point that the flow of change orders from the consultants will start, with the consultant claiming that the delay was beyond their control and therefore additional fees are required. If an event in your organization has caused a delay (which is not necessarily the same thing as additional work), you need to ask what the consultants were doing while waiting for a meeting to be scheduled, or an issue to be resolved or outstanding information to be received. Surely they were not sitting idly at their desks. Did they use the time to your benefit, and was what they worked on essential for the project?

Take a proactive approach to expected delay. Reduce the consulting resources so that you have fewer resources over a longer period, or ask the consulting firm to encourage the staff to take vacation, attend training, or participate in other non-chargeable activities while they wait for the delay to be resolved. This is certainly easier said than done, but it is important to have mechanisms in place to prevent consultants from automatically raising change orders every time there is a delay and to ensure that they are not working on nonproductive make-work activities that simply burn fees while they wait.

Accountability Cannot Be Transferred

The key message of the preceding discussion is that in the final analysis, the person who hired the consultants remains accountable for the performance of the project, even if they have used consultants to support the effort. As case study 11.2 illustrates, by accepting that accountability and putting in place a capable project manager who is an employee of the organization, you significantly increase the probability that you will realize value from the use of consultants in the overall project.

Case Study 11.2
CLIENT STRUCTURING AND MANAGING A PROJECT TO SUCCESS

A major U.S. company was very clear that the objective of their project was to launch a new product and that to do so they needed consultants with expertise in implementing a new system. The project was jointly managed and staffed, with the company only using consultants in roles that they did not have the capacity or capability to staff with internal resources. The company's project manager was very engaged in the day-to-day project management and met regularly with all the team leads, whether they were company staff or consulting staff. In other words, she did not simply attend a weekly meeting or read the one-page project status report.

The company's project manager understood that managing the scope was critical to the success of the project. The company also recognized that the system did not have to be perfect in order to support the business objective. Therefore, under the client project manager's direction, management made tough decisions about system functionality, proposing and accepting several compromises in order to meet the deadline. In the end, the client project manager was on the hook for the successful product launch and knew that it was her job to make sure the project succeeded; she could not simply leave this up to the consultants who could not judge which functionality was critical or not, and who could not successfully manage and communicate with all the stakeholders involved.

The company's approach resulted in strong teamwork, efficient communications, and a shared sense of responsibility between the company and their consultant. They would succeed or fail together. After the product was successfully launched, the company went on to implement more functionality and other products based on the same technology that they themselves had mastered during the course of the project.

Structuring a project is not necessarily difficult to do, but incorporating the insights gained from multiple experiences can certainly help you create an approach and a plan to avoid the many pitfalls that are likely to be encountered during project execution. However, you must be aware of the potentially very different perspectives consultants and their clients have regarding what defines success. Consultants will have a tendency to focus on the engagement. It is your job to ensure that they expand their view to include your broader business objectives for the project.

Management Summary

- Continually remember that the engagement is the basis upon which consultants define success while the project is what delivers value to your business. You need to bring the two definitions into alignment.

- Tie bonus payments to realization of the target project or business metrics.

- Projects should have a secondary benefit of increasing the capabilities of your organization's personnel by allowing them to participate in the work and to learn from the various approaches of consulting firms within their engagements.

- To maximize value from projects, roles should be assigned in a way that leverages the distinct competencies of each party.

- Be cautious of large-scale consulting projects in which the absolute number of consultants or the ratio of consultants to client personnel is large. It is better to break down such initiatives into manageable stages, even if implementation takes more time.

- To successfully realize your business objectives from projects that use consultants, you must be able to apply key project management principles and refrain from entirely outsourcing such responsibility to your consultants.

CHAPTER 12

RETAIN CONTROL OF YOUR CONSULTANTS

CONSULTANTS ARE HIRED WITH THE EXPECTATION THAT THEY WILL take direction from the executive, manager, and project manager in the organization. Yet paradoxically, once the consultants arrive, instead of just assisting, they start issuing instructions. In some ways, this is to be expected; consulting firms do most of their work on a project basis, whereas in most organizations the day-to-day operations are the primary focus and projects are something that is occasionally added to management's responsibilities. Thus, consultants are hired for their expertise in managing and executing projects. However, organizations should ensure that their consultants never lose sight of the fact that they are working at the behest of the client.

Consultants Report to You

Over the course of a project, especially a large one, it can be easy to forget what was actually proposed and contracted. Often, consulting firms will restructure work and shift activities into a subsequent phase after the commencement of their engagement. Periodically review current status and objectives relative to the original RFP, proposal, and contractual documents to keep everyone in alignment.

You need to manage your consultant as you would any direct report, being sure to:

- Establish clearly defined objectives, metrics, timelines, and expectations for how you want to work together.
- Understand the approach, work plan, and resources being utilized.
- Obtain regular updates outlining progress achieved, key obstacles, benefits realized, and upcoming activities.
- Review actual results achieved for resources deployed and fees and expenses incurred relative to budget and projections.

Minimize Change Orders

To manage change orders for consulting projects—especially those related to developing or implementing systems and that are priced on a fixed-fee basis—usually requires significant time and effort. The consultant may even dedicate a team member to this task. Expecting that there will be no change orders on a project is simply unrealistic. But managing change orders does not have to be as contentious as it often turns out to be. A well-defined scope and a detailed baseline plan are two essential underpinnings of the change control process. Beyond that it is important that all parties have agreed on a process in advance, whether the changes are identified and requested by you, the client, or whether the consultant raises them because they have been asked to take on work they consider out-of-scope. You will also need a proper way of estimating the impact of the change, not only on the consultant's fees but also on the project at large.

Speed is of the essence in making decisions on scope changes—especially if the scope change is really critical to the success of the project. Set up a regular meeting of all parties involved to discuss and decide on scope changes. Remember that the consultant is almost always going to agree to the scope changes if there is extra revenue involved. It will be up to the people from your organization who are involved in the scope control process to make tough decisions and, at times, reject change requests even though they may be raised by your own people. Few change control processes are designed to reject changes; they almost always assume the change will be approved. This should not be the case.

Change requests have been the downfall of many a project. Because they result in rework to incorporate the changes into deliverables that have already been completed, they increase the overall size, duration, complexity, and therefore risk of the project. Of greatest concern is that the additional cost is seldom evaluated against the original business case, so a project with a good business case at the outset may end up delivering much less value to the organization as the result of the incremental costs that were not considered at the start. And consulting firms will rarely raise change orders to reduce their fees if the original scope is reduced or planned functionality is removed; it will be up to you to identify these types of change orders.

Consultants are masters at identifying and justifying scope changes, which is often where the project margin is created. You need to become equally good at defining the scope up front and rejecting all but the most essential scope changes, no matter how well justified or well documented they are.

Engagements in Trouble

Though consultants may provide you with regular updates on a project, at face value the updates may not give you an accurate impression of the actual project status. You should look out for the following warning signs that your project could be in trouble.

DATA BUT NO INFORMATION

Lots of interviews have been conducted that are diligently minuted, but no conclusions have been drawn or deliverables produced. Ideally, information gathered should be rapidly incorporated into interim deliverables rather than recorded and filed as meeting minutes, waiting for someone to compile them into some type of deliverable weeks later. Meeting minutes are often simply a make-work exercise, and minutes without conclusions can mean that the persons involved in the meeting did not have the background to assimilate and assess the information, further meaning that the interview itself may have been a waste of time.

HUNTING IN PACKS

Consultants are always working in pairs and do not conduct meetings or interviews on their own. This usually means that one or both of them are weak and require backup. Considering their billing rates, this is not very cost-effective. An effective consultant should be able to conduct a meeting and take notes at the same time, without long pauses between each answer and the following question. If two people must conduct the interview, one of them should be from your organization—they should not both be consultants.

PROJECT MANAGER SPIN

If the project manager always responds to questions directed to specific consultants on the team, this is a sure sign that the project manager is covering for the consultants. Either she does not feel they are adequately performing their role, or she does not want them to inadvertently tell you what is really going on.

PROJECT MANAGER OUT OF TOUCH

If a project manager cannot respond to most of your questions without having to refer to a team member, he is not managing the project. A good project manager will have anticipated many of your questions and have the answers before you even raise them; he will not consistently have to defer to team members for answers.

FEES CONSUMED FASTER THAN WORK COMPLETED

When the percentage complete has not changed from one week to the next even though time has elapsed and fees have continued to be consumed, watch out! Issues may have arisen that consumed the consultants' time, but the engagement has not escalated the issues or expedited their resolution.

FALSE POSITIVE STATUS

There are many issues, warnings, and problems documented in the project status report, but the project manager still shows the overall status as green. This usually means that the consultant project manager is inexperienced and is not connecting the apparently isolated issues to the overall project status. Or perhaps the consultant does not want to trigger applicable escalation steps associated with a troubled project—either in your organization or the consulting firm—that a status other than green would precipitate.

SCOPE DIET

The consultant starts to define the scope more narrowly than originally agreed, eliminating departments to be interviewed, scaling back system functionality, or removing sections from deliverables. This is usually a sign that the original objectives cannot be met with the assigned resources in the agreed-upon time frame. Rarely do consultants submit scope changes or change requests to reduce the scope of the project and thus your fee invoice; they just keep working away with the assigned resources on an ever-shrinking scope.

BURNOUT

The project team is working a continuous stream of all-nighters. While this does happen occasionally on projects, it should not be the norm. A proper project plan should anticipate the lead time required to produce a deliverable for a final review, presentation, or implementation and should not schedule key activities right up until the last minute before a major deliverable is due.

MUTINY IN THE MAKING

An inexperienced or insecure consultant project manager may present everything to you as being under control even though his team may be overworked or abused. Though you may not perceive a situation in which the morale of the consultants is low and absentee rates are high to be your problem, it will be reflected in the end result of the project, which *is* your problem.

SURPRISE ENDINGS

Be concerned if you never see drafts of the deliverable nor participate in any discussions regarding its key ideas prior to the final presentation. If a deliverable is properly planned and well-crafted a significant amount of time will have been invested in validating the data and promoting the recommendations before the big day when everyone is formally seated in the boardroom.

WEAK CONCLUSIONS

If the information presented in formal deliverables is easily refuted by your management team, and recommendations are not well thought out and do not consider the reality of your situation, this may be because last-minute ideas have been injected by the partner on the day before the presentation. Or maybe the team is inexperienced and they have just copied recommendations from deliverables of other clients because they could not come up with their own.

THE BUCK STOPS AT THE PARTNER

If the partner does not have sufficient knowledge of the project to meet with you on their own, beware! As a client it is important that you insist on meeting with the partner or senior consulting representative on a regular basis to discuss the project. They should have sufficient knowledge of the project details to meet with you on their own. This allows you to raise issues that the project manager has not responded satisfactorily to. It also allows you to gauge how truly committed the partners or senior managers are to your project's success.

PROJECT, NOT CONSULTANT, MEETINGS

The consultant team should not have any reason to meet on their own without your team members. Excluding your team members from meetings is a sign that the consultants have their own agenda, or that there are issues they are not willing to share with the client members of the team. Also, for the project team to work effectively it should be fully integrated with client and consulting team members working under the same conditions and with the same information.

FOLLOW THE MONEY

Take special note of any deviations from the agreed-upon number of hours and fees. A regular and detailed review of any invoice presented is a must if you are to truly understand actual hours and expenses incurred (even if it is a fixed-fee project), and it will allow you to identify any deviations between planned hours and fees early on. Though it may not be productive to question immaterial expenses, you need to set and confirm at the outset that the standards are being monitored; otherwise, things can get out of control.

Avoid Being the Client from Hell

Every consultant has experienced a client from hell. These are the clients who the consultants run away from. You should avoid becoming known as such a client unless you want consultants who are less capable to be assigned to your project. This remains true no matter how disgruntled you might be with the partner or the consulting firm in general because they misrepresented the project or misled you about their capabilities. Remember that the consultants are there because you hired their firm, and they have been told to be there. Consultants deserve to be treated courteously, professionally, and with dignity. Junior consultants will go the extra mile, be more creative, and often not report the full extent of hours worked if they enjoy the client environment in which they are working (partly because they are enthralled by the work and partly because they know they are just learning and still cannot comprehend how much you are being charged for them). You are quite right to expect that they will be punctual, be well mannered, and display professional work habits, regardless of the actual quality of their output. If you are unhappy with an individual consultant, and you have the contractual option available, ask the partner to remove them from the project rather than making their life a living hell on a day-to-day basis.

Management Summary

- Be sure you remain in control of the consulting engagement by communicating your expectations up front and regularly thereafter.
- Manage your consultants as you would any direct report.
- Minimize change orders and move quickly when assessing them. Carefully consider whether or not change orders alter the scope of the engagement.
- Meet with the partner or senior manager of the consulting firm on a regular basis to sustain their interest and participation while drawing out their perspectives.
- Look out for warning signs that the consultants working on the engagement are in trouble.
- Treat consultants with professional courtesy regardless of what you think of their work.
- Consultant teams can easily assume a life of their own within your organization; you must remain in charge, manage their mandate, and be sure they understand where the boundaries lie.

CHAPTER 13

KNOW WHEN ENOUGH IS ENOUGH

"THE CONSULTANTS KNOW MORE ABOUT OUR BUSINESS AND INTERNAL politics than we do!" This is a familiar refrain from many a jaded employee. Are such comments unjustified or does perception represent reality? Some telltale signs that your consultants might have overstayed their welcome are these:

- Your consultants have easier access to you than your subordinates do.

- A consultant is present in most of your key management meetings.

- You immediately think of calling a consultant rather than one of your direct reports when you encounter a major challenge or problem, or you just want to bounce an idea off someone.

- The consultant has your mobile and home telephone numbers and calls you at all hours of the day and night.

- You have had the same consulting firm engaged on multiple projects continuously.

If any of the statements above are true for you, perhaps your consultants have become high-priced pseudo-employees. It is quite easy for business executives to fall into this trap.

Who Is Feeding the Frenzy?

Partners at most consulting firms seek to maximize the revenue stream from their current clients, and it is generally easier for consultants to sell more work to existing clients than to prospect for new clients. The path to partnership from the director or senior manager level at most consulting firms also depends on having a key client relationship that will continue to deliver revenue each year going forward; this justifies their admission to partnership. Global consulting firms have a list of target clients from whom they expect to generate the majority of their revenues. Thus, as case study 13.1 illustrates, cross-selling an ongoing series of engagements is an underlying objective of the majority of global consulting firms.

Case Study 13.1
CONSULTING FEEDING FRENZY

One of the largest companies in a particular industry sector in the United States proved to be fertile feeding grounds for at least half a dozen consulting firms. Over more than a century, the company had become a large, complex entity burdened with inefficient processes, a range of redundant processing centers, and multiple business unit fiefdoms. New management was determined to restructure the company in anticipation of an IPO a few years later. But the new management apparently had little confidence in their own employees, thereby creating the perfect environment for a consultants' feeding frenzy.

Progressively over a couple of years, one brand-name consulting firm leveraged an existing relationship to secure a series of projects aimed at reengineering all financial functions of the company. Another brand-name consultant addressed the redundant operations scattered around the country. A third firm attended to restructuring operations often overlapping with the second consulting firm. A fourth consulting company supported management with business strategy in the run-up to the IPO. A fifth one was brought in to build program management capabilities to keep track of all the projects and consultants. Eventually, consultants were interviewing other consultants rather than company employees about the workings of the company. At the various consulting firms, numerous senior managers "made partner," and entire industry-sector practices were built based on the huge amounts this one company was spending on consultants. This was a case of consultants getting out of control without proper management oversight being established nor periodic reviews being conducted to assess value realized.

Do Not Be a Consultant Junkie

Executives and managers can become dependent on consultants, partly because having an on-site consultant at your service is very convenient. Among other valuable services, they can:

- Provide research reports and the latest management thinking on a range of subjects.
- Rapidly research almost any topic by leveraging a global pool of analysts or consultants as well as having easy access to external research reports and databases.
- Present information succinctly by using structured communication approaches, graphical techniques, and professional graphic designers.
- Make additional manpower available at relatively short notice.
- Be an independent sounding board whose perspective isn't biased by the internal politics of your organization.

Consulting firms believe that their clients can obtain scale economies by reusing them for multiple assignments, as they do not need to relearn the business for every assignment but instead can leverage their institutional knowledge of the organization. However, buyers should recognize that

- Consulting resources do not typically stay on at one client's continuously, so the learning curve benefit is seldom realized. It is often only the partner—or the senior manager who is being considered for partnership—who is accumulating institutional knowledge and possibly transferring it to each new project team.

- Consultants are not a free or even low-cost resource but come at a premium price. Institutional knowledge may not justify the premium you are paying for it.

- Even if a consultant's services are offered free of charge, there is an agenda. Offering to undertake some research is usually a sales tactic, as the results of the "free research" or "free workshops" will typically identify or promote a large fee-generating opportunity for the consulting firm. If a "free" consultant is added to an existing project, the hope is that they will make themselves so indispensable that you agree to start paying for them at some point.

- By continuously going to your consultants rather than people in your own organization, you are not developing the capabilities of your own employees and strengthening your own business.

- Consultants do not always have the depth of expertise they profess even though a good consultant can "read the textbook" the night before or devise high-level frameworks to give you the impression they do. Thus, you may end up paying a premium for expertise that they do not actually have.

- Consultants may not be totally objective and independent; they do have other agendas or interests, such as revenue and staffing objectives, which may influence their advice.

- You may be limiting the influx of new ideas and approaches because consulting firms tend to promote their own point of view and execution approach. Over time, organizations and their consultants adopt similar lines of reasoning and solutions. Essentially, a new status quo emerges, undermining the effectiveness of the consultants in the organization.

- You can lose credibility with your people, because it may appear that you are reluctant to make business decisions without your preferred advisers.

Consultant Fatigue

Using the same consulting firm over consecutive years, even if it is on multiple projects, produces diminishing returns. After one or two years of using the same consulting firm, consultant fatigue usually sets in at the organization. Indeed, even using different consulting firms over multiple years can yield diminishing returns; your employees and management can get tired of providing the same information over and over again and having to explain why the latest management fad is not the miraculous solution to the company's business problems. It is therefore good practice to actively wean your organization off consultants periodically, preferably for a defined period of time, such as six months, one year, or more. One could even say that a benefit of a recession or business contraction cycle is that consulting budgets are invariably slashed, and companies are forced to learn how to do without consultants.

Cutting the Cord

It can be stressful to sever your dependency on a familiar consulting team. It may be accompanied by as much emotion as laying off a longtime employee, which is why we used the term "fire" in this book's subtitle. But this is particularly necessary when the consulting services have extended beyond their relatively narrow original scope or mandate. If there is no longer a reference point by which to judge the value of the consulting services being delivered, there will inevitably come a time when some higher-level executive or board member will ask about the true value being realized. This is one of the reasons why the selection of a consulting firm should be based on clearly defined criteria for each and every project. Otherwise, as illustrated in case study 13.2, the relationship can easily get out of control, destroying value for the organization.

Case Study 13.2

TOO MANY CONSULTANTS IS NEVER A GOOD THING

A multi-hundred-million-dollar open-ended contract between a major domestic company and a global consulting firm provided fertile ground for relationship selling, project overload, consultant fatigue, and declining value. The consulting firm was contracted for a multiyear commitment to assist the company with changing its business structure and revamping its business and technology systems. The contract was based on a few very high-level principles, with only the initial projects being roughly defined. As the number of consultants assigned to an ever-growing list of ill-conceived initiatives and projects multiplied, client employees increasingly began to question who was running the company and where the tangible business results from these never-ending consulting activities were. Over time, employees became disenfranchised; management became extensively distracted from its day-to-day business operations, given all the project demands and program management activity; and the required business results became more and more vague and illusive. Eventually, the consulting firm was dismissed prior to the completion of its contract (although they had already earned astronomical fees). The debacle contributed to the dismissal of the CEO and subsequently a few board members, while the company has yet to return to its former national stature.

The two case studies in this chapter illustrate the ease with which consulting expenditures can get out of control if releasing the consultants is not actively pursued by management. Consultant contractual relationships should never be open-ended. Consultants are simply one of many management tools and should be used in defined roles to achieve defined business objectives. Once the objectives have been achieved, the services should cease, and the organization's employees should resume managing the business.

To make it explicitly clear to consultants that your organization should not become the consulting firm's next target for a multiyear revenue stream, consider incorporating the following request into your RFP: "Describe the steps your consulting firm will take to actively disengage from our organization as you complete your commitments for this engagement." Their response should prove insightful and give you something to reference as you progress toward the end of the engagement with them.

Competitive Bids for Follow-on Work

The purchase of all consulting services should undergo an internal approval process before the contract can be awarded. There should be a high bar established to justify awarding significant follow-on or cross-sell projects to the same consulting firm without soliciting proposals from other firms. This avoids the tendency of project creep and creating a dependency on one consulting firm. If you notice a succession of approvals for consulting projects, perhaps you should determine the drivers for the continuous need for consultants. In some organizations, it may be more advantageous to build up an internal consulting team with the core skills required and supplement these with contractors or selected consultants to fill in the skill gaps as needed. Rather than engaging a full team of external consultants, periodically engaging specialist independent consultants to review projects, assess approaches, and challenge management's thinking could provide the objectivity and independence you require.

Again, it comes down to problem definition and specifying the roles to be filled and skill sets required to address that problem. You should not assume that all roles need to be filled by one external consulting firm. You should use some creativity in configuring projects made up of internal operational personnel, internal consultants, external contractors, and external consultants.

Orderly Shutdown

As the tenure of the consulting firm's engagement at your organization finally comes to an end, you should see that the following steps are taken:

- Compare what was finally delivered with what was promised in the original proposal and contract.

- Make sure your organization is provided with a descriptive inventory—maintained over the life of the project—of all documentation produced, including the supporting spreadsheets and associated material.

- Organize all documentation and ask for it to be provided in electronic and, if applicable, in hard-copy form.

- Identify personnel within your organization who, in the aggregate, can address any aspect of the project without the need to go back to the consultants. This should have been a natural outcome of the engagement team structure.

- Document your agreement with the consulting firm as to whether they can reference your project in any of their marketing and proposal materials, and if so, what they are allowed to say.

- See to it that all confidential material is returned to you and, if applicable, the consulting firm certifies that they have deleted all electronic or physical copies of the material.

Lessons Learned

Finally, when you bring a consultant assignment to closure, you should document your experiences in using that consultant. What role did they play? Did they discharge that role effectively relative to your expectations? What were the consultants particularly good at? Would you use them again? How would you use them differently? Too often, engagements end without the client doing an effective postmortem to identify lessons learned so that consultants can be used more effectively the next time. If you have centralized consulting procurement personnel they should actively participate in the debriefing process so that they can take the lessons learned and apply them on projects in other parts of the organization. See chapter 16 and appendixes 4 and 5 for further information on post-project reviews.

Consultants are not an inexpensive proposition, so you, as the buyer of consulting services, must ensure that you become more effective over time at extracting the value they promise.

Brutal Honesty

Once a project is under way and the consultant is engaged, most of the parties involved will do their best to bring a project to conclusion and communicate its outstanding success. The consulting firm will wish to update their qualifications list with another "home run" engagement. Within the organization that hired the consultants, the management team who approved the project, the sponsor of the project, the team that selected the consultants, the project manager, and the project team all have careers that are staked on the project being a great success. That is fortunate for consultants because, more often than they would like to admit, their engagements do not realize the project's originally intended business objectives even if the consultant's engagement was completed and something was delivered. This "false positive" outcome is an internal management issue that organizations rarely acknowledge. But in order to extract value from consultants on future engagements, you will have to make sure that you are brutally honest within your organization when reflecting on the project.

Management Summary

- It can be very easy for the unwitting executive or manager to become dependent on consultants. This is an explicit objective of most consulting firms and they will subtly (and sometimes not so subtly) take steps to increase your dependency on them.

- While there are advantages to leveraging the same consulting firm on an ongoing basis, they should be weighed against the disadvantages of a declining value proposition that may lead to consultant fatigue and the establishment of a new status quo.

- To avoid dependency, executives and managers should be proactive and periodically cease the use of their consultants, or even try to do some projects without any consulting firm's participation.

- Get consultants to deliver a detailed plan for disengaging from an assignment.

- All requests for expenditure on consulting services should undergo an internal approval process with a higher bar applied to awarding follow-on engagements without a competitive bidding process.

- All requests for expenditures on consulting services should undergo an internal approval process with a higher bar applied to awarding follow-on engagements without a competitive bidding process.

- Be creative in structuring approaches to solve business problems without necessarily always defaulting to hiring full teams of external consultants.

- Oversee the orderly shutdown of any consultant engagement.

- Be sure to document the lessons you have learned from using consultants to bring closure to the engagement and improve the value you can obtain from them in the future.

CHAPTER 14

IN THE EVENT OF TERMINATION

THERE ARE TIMES WHEN AN ENGAGEMENT CANNOT CONTINUE TO A successful conclusion, possibly preventing the completion of the project itself and the realization of long-awaited business benefits. There are two types of circumstances under which engagements end prematurely:

1. Circumstances beyond the control of the consultant: Due to a change in business direction the project is terminated, along with any consulting and related vendor contracts.

2. Circumstances under the control of the consultant: The consultant has not performed according to your expectations or has not met their contractual obligations, so you terminate the contract, which may also result in the overall project being canceled. This also includes the rare case in which a consultant exercises their right to exit the engagement.

If you or your legal advisers addressed these two scenarios in your contract, the contractual steps to be taken under either type of circumstance should be clearly outlined there. But the practical steps that you need to take almost certainly will not be.

Change in Business Environment

Some projects make perfect sense when initially conceived, but a lot can happen in the business environment in a short time, such as regulatory changes, mergers, acquisitions, or a change of key personnel in your management team. Sometimes, these changes in the business environment will require you to take stock of your existing project inventory and determine which projects no longer make sense. A change in expected value from a project could come from the realization that the premise for undertaking the project was incorrect or from subsequent information that reveals the business objectives will not benefit the business to the extent anticipated in the planning stage. Sometimes projects are terminated simply because the funds or resources being tied up in the project could be put to better use elsewhere in the organization.

Terminating the Consultant Without Cause

In cases where the reason for terminating the project has nothing to do with the performance of the consultant, such as a change in business direction or failures to fulfill your own obligations on the project, your consultants will be understanding. They recognize that these things happen. In fact, they are usually astute enough to read the signs before you tell them anything is up—although they may not say anything in the hope that the inevitable will be delayed so that their revenue stream is preserved for a bit longer.

If you recall, a key element of the economic model of consulting firms is to minimize non-billable time, particularly idle gaps between projects. Consulting firms have people, systems, and processes for scheduling staff. This allows them to predict staff availability—based on the dates that consultants are scheduled to roll off existing engagements, among other things—and actively work to reassign them, thus constantly maximizing overall staff utilization. Partners and schedulers start planning how to redeploy staff well in advance of the date they are expected to complete their current assignment. Therefore, if a client terminates a project or engagement unexpectedly, the consulting firm expects to receive compensation to cover a reasonable interval during which they anticipate not being able to redeploy the staff. Depending on what you had agreed to in your contract, you may be required to provide a paid notice period to the consultant. This notice period, which typically is subject to negotiation as to whether the consultants work during this time or not, is designed to cover the dip in revenues that the abrupt termination of a whole team of people would bring.

Other than resolving the notice period issue, the project should be closed down in the same way as any project coming to a normal end (see coverage in chapter 13), also taking care of the communications and stakeholder management considerations described later in this chapter.

Termination of a Troubled Project

Organizations do not cancel troubled projects often enough. Management often seems to find it easier to keep listening to all the problems (believing and hoping that next month the project will catch up) and to defer dependent business activities (product launches, system rollouts, etc.) than to walk away. Sometimes, this is because completing the project is an imperative, and there is no perceived alternative to continuing. But when the project was optional in the first place, management rarely decides that they should take an immediate, certain loss rather than waiting for a future, probable failure. Even if the project was imperative, sometimes the best course of action involves continuing the project without the assistance of the consulting firm that was selected for the project. Under these circumstances you will need, and should already have negotiated the right, to terminate the consulting contract. The only question is to what extent lawyers will be involved. The answer depends on whether you consider the consulting firm to be legally responsible for the delays or issues affecting the project.

Terminating the Consultant for Cause

If you are terminating the engagement because the consultant has not kept up their end of the bargain, and if you expect to get any relief in the courts in terms of refund of fees paid or other compensation, you will have to have a well-documented timeline of events and supporting documents. The documents will need to show the series of failures or actions on the part of the consultant and their unwillingness or inability to rectify such failures. Every case is different, as is each jurisdiction, but any legal action on your part will require an extensive amount of effort and will involve a significant time commitment from internal or external counsel. Apart from the satisfaction of proving that the consulting firm let you down, the legal remedies will usually be slow in coming and will invariably not compensate you for the lost project time and the inability to realize the expected business benefits in the required time frame. This is why it is so important to make sure you select the right consultant from the start and that you figure out how to manage and work through issues with them.

If the project has become a battleground, and finger-pointing and risk mitigation have distracted the consultants from the job they were hired to do, your best bet after following pre-agreed escalation steps and requesting a change of key people, including the partner if necessary, is to terminate the engagement if it is an option. A bad relationship rarely improves under the pressure of a project environment. Your strongest negotiating chip for recovering fees from the consulting firm is the threat of publicity that a lawsuit would bring, because the consulting firm will be anxious to avoid the dispute becoming a public matter and damaging their reputation.

Extracting compensation for damages is another matter altogether, and most consulting firms will resist admitting fault in such circumstances unless the scenarios and remedies are explicitly laid out in the contract, which most major consulting firms are pretty good at avoiding. Regardless, no amount of lawyering will allow you to begin the project over again with a different consultant and still get the originally intended benefits at the original cost. You will have already lost.

Firing Individual Consultants

Hopefully, you negotiated the right to request that an individual on the team be replaced in an orderly manner if their performance (quality of work, professionalism, output rate, etc.) or skill is not meeting your project requirements. In these cases, a conversation with the partner should take care of it. The partner will then tell the consultant to pack up, and if required, propose a replacement. The fact that you don't have to manage these types of HR and staff issues is one of the joys of hiring consultants.

You will need to make sure that there is an orderly transition of the consultant's work to someone else; that the partner explains the situation to the remaining consultants; and that you communicate with your internal staff to avoid rumors and morale dips that could impact the rest of the team's performance.

Consultant Terminating the Contract

In very rare cases (rare because consulting firms usually do not leave money on the table), a consulting firm may have the right to terminate the contract. Usually, the circumstances are related to force majeure or other major catastrophes that simply make it impossible for them to carry out their obligations under the contract. In some extreme circumstances, a consulting firm may determine that they are unable to fulfill the obligations of the project and that it would be better for them to simply withdraw from the engagement, possibly offering to refund some of your fees. This could occur if they mispriced the project, discover your environment is significantly different from what they were made to understand, or find the atmosphere too hostile and not conducive to a successful outcome. In most cases, the consulting firm will have embedded within the contract termination clauses for themselves, and if you agreed to the clauses, there is almost nothing you can do to convince the firm to reconsider their decision to end the relationship. For this reason, it is important that they have a contractual obligation to transition their project responsibilities to your staff or a third party in an orderly manner.

Communications and Stakeholder Management

When projects go wrong, people from both sides will have an interest in working to minimize the visibility and fallout. Why the consulting firm would be motivated to do this is obvious. But the internal team involved in the selection of the consulting firm and the management of the project will also hasten to distance themselves from the debacle to avoid being implicated in the failure. Because of this, most failed projects and engagements are quietly swept under the rug. Very large projects that get canceled will probably be mentioned in the press, especially if the public is already aware of the project. If this is your unfortunate situation, your marketing and public relations people must have sufficient notice of the project cancellation so they can plan how to respond (or not) to calls from the media. The consulting firm will also be doing their best to manage the message in order to limit damage to themselves. Luckily, most projects that get canceled are not that big or that famous, but most will still trigger an internal witch hunt and generate some internal public relations issues that will have to be dealt with.

Management Summary

- Internal and external self-interests keep projects in play and often promote the perception of greater engagement and project success than what was actually realized. Thus, while many consulting engagements are indeed concluded successfully, termination rarely happens for those that are failing to realize the originally expected business objectives.

- Terminations without cause are usually driven by changes impacting the organization that are outside the control of the consultant. The client and consultants can typically manage these terminations in an orderly manner. The primary negotiating point is usually the paid notice period to the consultants as they expect to be compensated for the unexpected decline in utilization.

- Terminations for cause rarely result in a satisfactory outcome—the organization falls further behind in realizing its business benefits while the consulting firm fights to protect its reputation and avoid legal liability. At best, depending on the severity of the breach and the documentation trail of the issues, organizations may secure compensation or the refund of some or all of the fees paid. At worst, if clear scenarios and penalties were not defined in the contract, protracted legal proceedings will result in little satisfaction, leaving the organization no closer to realizing the required business benefit.

- Be aware that you usually have the right to terminate individuals on the consulting team if they are not meeting your expectations.

- Understand that consultants terminate contracts in some very rare cases. Consultants may terminate for internal reasons, miscalculations of the project's required resources, or incompatibility with the client company. Make sure you have a mechanism for a smooth project transition if the consultant terminates.

- Be proactive in involving your internal communication department to manage the messages to internal and external stakeholders as a result of a terminated project.

CHAPTER 15

HOW TO UNDERMINE THE EFFECTIVENESS OF YOUR CONSULTANTS

BY READING THE PRECEDING CHAPTERS YOU WILL HAVE DEVELOPED an understanding of the inner workings of the consulting business; understood the differences in the economic models of the various types of consulting firms; become aware of some of the consulting tricks of the trade; and learned how to select, manage, and release consultants. By this stage, any friendships that we, the authors, had established within the consulting industry no longer exist. But perhaps we can win those friends back. As outlined at the beginning of this book, the fault for realizing poor value from consultants often lies not with the consulting firm, but with the organization that hired them in the first place.

For those of us in the consulting profession, it never ceases to amaze us that organizations hire high-priced consultants and then do not create an environment in which they can be effective. The following outlines just some of the practices you should apply if you really wish to undermine the effectiveness of your consultants and limit the value they can deliver. We do hope that the real-life situations described make you chuckle as you shake your head in disbelief at how poorly other companies utilize their consultants.

Present Logistic Challenges to Test the Most Creative of Consultants

CRAM EIGHT CONSULTANTS INTO A ROOM DESIGNED FOR TWO PEOPLE

This is the old telephone booth experiment for those of us who remember it as beer-drinking adolescents. Despite the large skyscrapers or vast factory floors that organizations occupy, office space always seems to be at a premium. Nothing gets a project off to a good start like an engagement team showing up, excited to take on the key strategic challenges of their client, only to find that for the duration of the project they will be packed into a small room that quickly becomes an oven from the heat generated by their bodies and laptops. Under these circumstances, the choices are for the consultants to be unproductive at their client site or to incur much unproductive travel time going back and forth to their consulting office. This approach to providing office space for consultants also undermines the ability to integrate internal personnel and consultants within the project team thereby reducing knowledge transfer, execution effectiveness, and buy-in. You are paying good money for consultants, so help them be productive by making sufficient space available for them and colocating them with your own employees.

DO NOT PROVIDE ANY MEETING ROOMS

As independent outsiders, consultants can encourage your management and employees to be more open with them in articulating the issues and challenges facing the organization. However, open-plan offices are not conducive to candor. Because consultants undertake a significant number of interviews and frequently meet to debrief, brainstorm, or debate in the course of an assignment, the availability of meeting rooms is a critical component of productivity.

DO NOT PROVIDE ACCESS TO EMAIL, INTERNET, AND PRINTING FACILITIES

Consultants need to conduct research on their internal and external databases, email requests for information and guidance, and exchange perspectives with subject matter experts elsewhere in their firm. They also need to exchange information with your staff, ideally on your email system to minimize concerns about confidential information leaving your organization. During the course of the project, the consultants will also need to periodically print meeting minutes, interim documents, and final deliverables for review by you and your managers. It can be very unproductive if they have to continually hand a thumb or flash drive to a secretary in order to print files. Although still not optimal, on many occasions consultants have had to resort to buying personal printers for client sites due to the unavailability of printing facilities; however, these are usually good just for short draft documents. It is much more productive if you make email, Internet, and network printing facilities available for your consultants before they arrive; otherwise, this will be another reason for them not to work at your site, in which case you will have already given up some control of the project.

DO NOT PROVIDE ANY ADMINISTRATIVE SUPPORT

Do you really want a US$200-an-hour junior consultant or the US$450-an-hour project manager attending to the logistics of scheduling a series of meetings and booking conference rooms within your vast organization? Consulting firms have no problem providing administrative support; after all, you are paying them. However, it is probably better to assign a part-time assistant to help them get such rudimentary tasks as these done more cost-effectively.

Present Overwhelming Execution Challenges

KEEP CHANGING THE BUSINESS OBJECTIVES AND SCOPE OF WORK

Consultants define the approach, number, type of consultants, and time frame based on the scope of work and the business objectives you originally stated. Change the scope or business objectives and they usually will need to replan; this often results in an adjustment to resources or duration, with time being lost during the transition from one approach to the other. If you make such changes constantly, the consultants will not build up momentum and the project will likely cost you significantly more than you budgeted. The team may also become confused and find it hard to follow what the latest objective is. The result is muddled, out-of-date, and hastily put together deliverables. Some change is inevitable, but be conscious that changes come with a price.

WITHHOLD PROMISED RESOURCES

It can be exceedingly difficult to free up resources in large enterprises. But if the consulting team had incorporated your resources into their plan, and such resources do not eventuate when planned, the consultants will be handicapped from the perspectives of manpower, orientation, and intellectual contributions. They will then have to either make do without these additional resources or supplement the team with additional consultants, picking up whoever is on the bench at their office even though they may not be the best fit for the role.

ASSIGN YOUR POOR PERFORMERS TO THE PROJECT TEAM

Even worse is when departments in your organization, pressured to assign resources to a consulting project, place their weakest performers on the team. Not only does this negatively impact the team from an output perspective, it also actually taxes the consulting team. They become a group of high-priced babysitters dreaming up work to keep the hapless employee busy with tasks that will not put the consultant's deliverables at risk. In addition, because the capability gap between the consultants, who have usually graduated as top-ranked students, and the poor performer is often large, the blow to morale taken by the poor performer occasionally results in that person bad-mouthing the project. If you want a good, value-added outcome then you need to assign good, value-adding people.

EXECUTIVES PLAY "HIDE AND SEEK" WITH THE CONSULTANTS

There is nothing so frustrating as when a consultant faces a tight deadline demanded by their client sponsor, yet the executives and employees they need to meet with are unavailable for days or even weeks, making it impossible to meet deadlines. This "unavailability" could be because your executives were improperly briefed as to the importance and timeline of the project; they are being passive-aggressive because they do not support the project; or they are simply poor managers of their time.

FORGET THE TICKING CLOCK

Most consultants understand that they are on the clock, but clients often forget and lose focus. Sure, spend some time bantering and relaying personal stories to build rapport and take the edge off the day-to-day business pressures. In some cultures, these interactions are essential in order to build sufficient trust and to draw out perspectives. But making consultants wait outside your office for thirty minutes is not a productive use of their time or your consulting dollars. Nor is making them listen to you talk on the phone for fifteen minutes of the meeting they had scheduled with you.

HIRE ANOTHER CONSULTING FIRM TO OVERSEE YOUR CONSULTANTS

Consulting firms are competitive. Asking one consulting firm to provide oversight of another not only puts you one step further away from the project but also wastes your and your consultants' time; they will likely be constantly trying to score points off one another or blaming each other for project issues, and you will have to be the referee. Some of this may not necessarily be deliberate; different consulting firms have different approaches to solving problems and therefore may simply not be able to get in sync with each other. Hire a consultant to do your job and you are only inviting problems.

Present Participation Challenges That Limit the Effectiveness of the Consultant Work Team

BE UNAVAILABLE OR UNPREPARED FOR UPDATE AND STEERING COMMITTEE MEETINGS

Preparing for steering committee meetings typically entails considerable time and effort. Furthermore, it involves high-priced business executives' and consultants' time and usually requires confirmation of facts presented, perspectives on how to overcome obstacles, and decisions to be made on a number of key business topics. Executives need to actively listen, seek clarification, and challenge the consultants on their findings and recommendations. Too often, consultants make presentations to executives who are passively listening, without an apparent opinion. Executives are not supposed to switch off when the consultants arrive; they should not assume that the consultants know exactly what they are doing or have all the answers. Consultants do sometimes take a best guess as to the approach, and if they are not challenged by the client they will continue down a path that perhaps takes them, and you, in the wrong direction.

DELAY DECISIONS

There is no better way to undermine the value of consultants than to procrastinate, particularly when a team of them is waiting for a decision to be made before they can proceed with their next task. Given the high incidence of this, some consulting firms include terms in their contracts to the effect that any delays arising from indecision will result in incremental elapsed time and consulting fees. Sure, the consultants must thoroughly research and provide the cost benefits of different options, but sooner rather than later management must make a decision on which direction to take.

FAIL TO ASSIGN ACCOUNTABILITY FOR EXECUTING THE NEXT STEPS

Ideally, over the course of the project it will become apparent which of your people on the project will drive the next steps after the consultants leave. But too often this does not occur. The report is presented, the original sponsoring executive has a new role elsewhere in the organization, and there is no one tasked with moving the result to the next step—implementation. This happened at a large U.S.-based company, where a consulting firm completed their engagement, but the company failed to effectively assign responsibility for and to continue with the implementation. Four years later, after departmental management had changed, the company undertook the same project again, using the same consulting firm, which came up with basically the same recommendations. It was good for the consulting firm since they got paid to do the same assignment twice, but poor value for the company.

BE PENNY WISE, POUND FOOLISH BY RELEASING YOUR CONSULTANTS TOO SOON

While organizations should take responsibility for their projects, occasionally at the end of the project it is clear that they do not have a person with the right skill set available to take the necessary next steps. However, in order to minimize expenditure on consultants, organizations do not retain one or two consultants to sustain momentum until an internal person can be assigned or the next steps have been completed. The pace of progress declines and results in a reduced set of benefits being realized much later than planned, if at all. Figuring out whether consulting support is really needed beyond the end of the initial engagement can be a challenge, but it comes back to first principles. You need to reassess and define what the problem is at that point, decide which roles need to be filled, and determine whether your organization can fill such roles.

Strategies That Will Alienate the Consultants Within Your Organization

DO NOT SECURE MANAGEMENT AND ORGANIZATIONAL BUY-IN TO THE PROJECT

This approach is much more common than you would think. You believe consultants are an important component to move an initiative forward, but others on your management team or elsewhere in the organization are dubious about the need for the project and particularly the need for consultants. This often happens between local operations and their regional or global head offices. Executives in those central organizations are frequently confident that they can simply dictate to their business units what needs to be done, whether it is to support an initiative, implement a system, or adopt a standard. The resulting resistance, often evidenced in passive-aggressive behavior, almost guarantees that any project, even with the right consulting approach, will not be as successful as it could have been. The approach that a senior executive uses to enroll the consultant in a new project initiative is often just as important as the project itself in determining the level of success of an initiative and the value you realize from the consultants.

DO NOT INFORM SOME MEMBERS OF YOUR MANAGEMENT AND ORGANIZATION ABOUT THE PROJECT

Organizations engage a consulting firm but sometimes fail to communicate to their broader organization the purpose, role, and time frame for the use of the consultants. The first time some employees hear about the project is when one of the consultants contacts them, looking for information. Delays ensue while the employee confirms that the request is legitimate, complains about not being informed, and suggests other approaches to the project. And generally, the consultant is given a hard time for doing the job they were hired to do. Yes, consultants do have rather thick skin, but sometimes even their performance suffers when they are treated unreasonably.

MAKE DEROGATORY COMMENTS ABOUT CONSULTANTS TO YOUR STAFF

If you have hired consultants then you must commit to the decision. If you, as the client, are making derogatory comments about the approach, experience level, or fees associated with the consultants you hired, you will not promote buy-in to the consultants or any of their recommendations, thereby undermining the reason you hired them in the first place.

Create an Environment for Success

Organizations can spend significant time defining their problem, determining the roles a consultant should fill, and following a rigorous selection and contracting process. But consultants can be effective and deliver greater levels of value only if the right working environment is created for them from day one within your organization. Many of the factors that reduce the efficiency of consultants are logistical in nature and relatively easy to address. Other factors have to do with the support provided for executing project tasks. However, sustaining timely, active management participation and promoting organizational buy-in are probably the most difficult for the consultants to contend with.

Extracting value from consultants has as much to do with the environment you create for the consultants as it does with the selection, management, and release of consultants.

Management Summary

- Don't let such productivity-sapping logistical issues as availability of office space and meeting rooms, access to Internet and printing, and administrative support hinder your consultants' effectiveness.
- Execution issues—changing objectives and scope, assigning resources, timely availability of executives, and avoiding conflict between consulting firms—require your proactive effort to ensure that they do not impact the consultant's productivity.

- Participation problems (e.g., management engagement in steering committees, challenging consultants in review meetings, making timely decisions, or assigning accountability) can require some extra guidance and direction from you to keep your own organization on track.

- Buy-in problems, such as management team support, communication to organization, and personal comments, can usually be anticipated and mitigated with advanced actions.

MANAGING CONSULTANTS FOR SUCCESS

CONSULTANTS UNDOUBTEDLY CAN PLAY MANY ROLES AND PROVIDE significant value to any business. The consulting profession would not have been so successful if this were not the case. However, as outlined at the start of this book, the degree of value received is to a large extent determined by you, the buyer, in effectively selecting and managing your consultants so as to extract the potential value from them.

Here is a reminder of some of the reasons why consultants do not deliver adequate value:

- The consultants are working on the wrong problem.
- You have selected the wrong type of consultants for the problem at hand.
- The consultants doing the work do not have the skills or experiences that were proposed.
- You are not using or managing the consultants effectively.
- The consultants have lost their effectiveness in your organization.

Over the course of reading this book, you should have developed a much better understanding of the economics of the consulting model;

how that model drives the behavior and incentives for partners and consultants within consulting firms; and the potential impact this may have on the way they market, sell, and deliver services within your organization. You should also have developed an appreciation of how to manage your consultants through the selection, delivery, and releasing stages, allowing you to avoid the shortcomings while permitting you to secure greater value from consultants.

We conclude this book by restating our view that extracting value from consultants depends on two parties:

1. First, you the client, in the manner you select, manage, and disengage your consultants; and

2. Second, the consultants themselves, in terms of the integrity and capability of their partners and employees to assist in defining and solving the problem.

Accordingly, you should evaluate the performance of both your organization and of your consultants. To help you do this evaluation, forms are provided in appendixes 4 and 5. The first is an organization evaluation. This covers the steps you, the buyer of consulting services, should complete internally to assist your organization to extract value from consultants for a particular project. The questions are drawn from the principles in this book and assume that you have read the book to understand the details. To maximize the benefit of this evaluation, complete the selection section as soon as possible after you have completed the selection process, and then complete the rest at the end of the engagement.

The second is a consultant evaluation for you to document how well your consultants performed. This questionnaire allows you to summarize your experience in using a particular consultant for a particular project.

If you would like to benchmark your experience with consultants against other organizations' experiences you can do so by completing the consultant evaluation form online at our website:

www.ExtractValueFromConsultants.com

After considering all the positive and negative aspects of working with consultants, we believe these statements to be true:

- Consultants have the potential to deliver immeasurable value to make your business more successful.
- The value you extract from consultants is very much under your control, and evaluating your use of consultants on an ongoing basis will allow you to improve your effectiveness at extracting that value over time.

By applying the principles and practices we have recommended, you will be well equipped to extract the most value from your consultants in order to realize greater success for both yourself and your company.

APPENDIX 1

BEWARE: CONSULTING IS DIFFERENT IN ASIA

IN THE TWENTY-FIRST CENTURY, ASIA HAS EMERGED AS THE REGION with the most significant economic growth opportunities. Its average annual gross domestic product (GDP) growth rates are well above those of North America or Western Europe. This shift in focus of economic activity away from North America and Europe toward Asia will continue throughout this century. At the turn of the century, Asia accounted for 26 percent of global GDP. The International Monetary Fund forecasts this will grow to 36 percent by 2014, while the United States' share of global GDP, which was 25 percent in the year 2000, will fall to 18 percent. For businesses based in Asia, as well as for global multinationals whose home offices are based outside Asia, the region represents a key strategic area for future growth in revenues and profits. Given this rapid economic growth and the current scarcity of management talent, demand for consulting services in Asia has exploded. Yet, finding consulting firms to support Asian operations presents some unique challenges. Companies in Asia that are seeking value from consultants must be aware of these challenges in order to make the best choice when hiring a consultant.

Consulting Is a Well-Established Industry in the West

Within the large markets of the United States and Canada, where the consulting profession originated about a hundred years ago, consulting firms have developed a deep bench of consultants, covering all industry sectors and competencies at each level of the pyramid. There may be gaps in one city or subregion, but due to the homogeneity of language and culture it is easy to fill client demands by flying in resources or specialists from another city or subregion that has the capacity or requisite expertise. In fact, in North America it is quite common for consultants who live on the West Coast to work at a client's site on the East Coast while East Coast–based consultants of the same firm commute to the West Coast for the duration of their assignment. The consulting market is mature, has scale within a country, and has a history of delivering capable resources on a reasonably consistent basis.

Europe's greater fragmentation in terms of labor regulations, languages, and culture occasionally creates some challenges. For example, on a project for a client in Switzerland, the project manager had difficulty getting consultants from the German practice to work on-site five days a week, although the consultants from the UK practice of the same global firm did this as a matter of routine. Although these types of differences do exist, European nations are similar enough to allow for some movement of consulting resources within Europe and between Europe and North America. This ability to share resources across borders in Europe is also aided by greater multilingual capabilities among the general populace, the use of English as a common business language on the continent, and for many countries, a common economic zone obviating the need for work visas.

Asia Is Different

Asia is an entirely different matter. Consulting firms started operations there relatively recently. Local businesses do not fully understand, appreciate, or value consultants. Most local executives are comfortable with more tangible products such as physical computers and consumer commodities, things they can see and touch, rather than intangible services such as concepts and ideas on pages of a report.

In some Asian countries, it is considered an admission of failure on the part of the CEO or senior executive to use management consultants. The demand for consulting services in many countries is limited to the multinationals and a few large domestic companies and is therefore insufficient to build critical mass within each and every country. On the supply side, consulting is a relatively new profession for Asian students to consider entering and is not as highly regarded as careers in finance, medicine, or engineering. As a consequence, consulting firms in Asia do not necessarily attract the best talent in the region. All these factors may account for the absence of any large Asian-based consulting firms—other than sizable local technology consultants and the global India-based firms—and why the consulting choices for organizations in Asia are largely limited to foreign-based firms.

Cultural Considerations

Business leaders in Asia will find that consulting firms do not adjust their delivery model to reflect the region's vast cultural differences. Those cultural differences, and the impacts they have on the business environment, have been well documented by several academics. *The Culture Advantage* (Intercultural Press, 2006) by M. Huijser and *When Cultures Collide* (Nicholas Brealey Publishing, 1996) by R.D. Lewis are two outstanding works. One of the most famous studies was undertaken by Geert Hofstede and published under the title *Culture's Consequences* (Sage Publications, 2001) and later updated in *Cultures and Organizations* (McGraw-Hill U.S.A., 2004). He identified five dimensions of culture that vary across countries (see figure A1.1). Organizations in Asia can benefit from studying Dr. Hofstede's work in order to understand how Western-based consulting firms will relate to their culture.

Cultural Tendencies Drive Business Behavior

Figure A1.1 depicts a series of spider charts based on data from Hofstede surveys that profile the cultural tendencies of eleven countries. India, in the middle, also serves as the legend, showing which cultural dimension each axis represents. The five cultural dimensions are:

a. Comfort with power status: acceptance of the hierarchy as the source of power

b. Masculinity: the gap between men's values and women's values reflecting the distribution of roles between the genders

c. Individualism: preference for working, identifying, and being rewarded as an individual, rather than as part of a group

d. Uncertainty avoidance: extent toward which actions and decisions are taken in order to avoid dealing with ambiguity or unknown risks

e. Long-term orientation: actions and decision are more oriented to long-term than short-term results

Figure A1.1: Relative Cultural Tendencies for Selected Countries

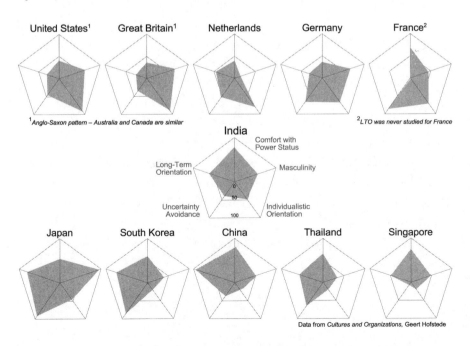

Data from *Cultures and Organizations*, Geert Hofstede

While research into cultural tendencies has stoked much debate, the key insight when looking across different countries is that cultures do vary, and these variations are exhibited in people's behavior in the workplace. Accordingly, organizations must look for consultants who are sensitive to potential differences between their culture and the client's, and who are aware of how those differences may impact the way client's staff within a particular culture (a) perceive their business environment; (b) relate to their superiors, peers, and subordinates; (c) interpret spoken and written information; (d) devise solutions to problems; and (e) determine the best way to implement those solutions. Europeans tend to be more intuitively sensitive to cultural differences than North Americans are, but remember, North America is where most global consulting firms originate!

As shown, countries with an Anglo-Saxon heritage (United States, United Kingdom, Australia, and Canada), which are where consulting firms have their strongest historical roots, have fairly consistent cultural tendencies. People from Anglo-Saxon countries tend to have less tolerance of hierarchical power (particularly if it is not earned), balance career advancement with personal and family aspirations, and are more individualistic, risk taking, and short-term oriented compared to people from many other countries. Continental European countries, from the small sample shown, are less homogeneous and appear to have a greater diversity of cultural tendencies.

Cultural tendencies for countries within Asia, six of which have been depicted in figure A1.1, have a remarkably different pattern from those of Anglo-Saxon countries. They also vary considerably in relation to each other.

Consulting Skills Assume Western Cultural Tendencies

As a generalization, there is a tendency in Asia toward longer-term orientation, a desire for group cohesiveness, and a respect for ascribed power, that is, power that arises from the age, position, or institutional affiliation of the individual who leads on the basis of networks and personal experiences. In Anglo-Saxon countries, by contrast, there is a greater tendency to challenge authority through constructive inquiry and rational problem solving rather than to simply accept statements reflecting the wisdom of elders. Some Asian cultures—Japan and South Korea, in particular—have a high desire for certainty and are therefore likely in business to look for solutions based on proven success, requesting consultants to implement "best practices." Western facilitation techniques to draw out information and perspectives in a workshop setting are not often effective in Asia since respect for seniority will cause the junior personnel in a workshop to remain silent, particularly given the greater personal risk of speaking out and the desire not to appear individualistic in a group setting.

If a consulting firm has not recognized the need to adapt their sales and delivery techniques for each country in Asia and trained their Asian and Western staff accordingly, they will not be successful in delivering value to you. And for them, adapting is difficult because the foundational skills required by the Western models of management consulting are not necessarily consistent with the cultural norms of their Asian staff. To close the gap between the naturally agreeable approach of Asian consulting staff and the more assertive demeanor sometimes required to effectively deliver consulting services requires adaptation of both the consulting approach itself and intense behavior-modification training not usually required by Western-based consultants.

In most firms there are a few Asian consultants who have managed to progress up the ladder to partner, sometimes at such an accelerated rate that they miss a few years of valuable experience because of battlefield promotions or some strategic title-inflating job changes. In spite of this, their numbers are still insufficient to institutionalize the adaptation needed from Western to Asian consulting approaches in their respective global firms.

Organizations in Asia have to satisfy themselves that the consulting firm has recognized and successfully implemented the adaptations necessary to be effective within their specific market. As case study A1.1 illustrates, lack of awareness of cultural differences can lead to failed projects.

Case Study A1.1

PROJECT IGNORED CULTURAL TENDENCIES AND DIFFERENCES

A UK-based software development company successfully sold their application system to a midsize company based in Thailand. The software was really a shell that needed detailed user requirements to be specified before functionality could be built. The UK office did not have an operation in Thailand, so they flew their consultants to Bangkok to interview the client staff through translators, supplemented with Thai business analysts who were unfamiliar with the product. The first problem was that the UK consultants were unaware that the constructs of the Thai language do not explicitly differentiate between past, present, and future, so it proved difficult for the UK consultants to ascertain whether statements made reflected what the current system did or what they wanted the new system to do. Second, people of Thailand have a strong respect for hierarchy and generally avoid confrontation; as a result, the Thai personnel were not predisposed to challenge the UK consultants who, after all, presented themselves as experts.

Another issue was that, given the Thai preference for certainty, once the first module of the system was built and tested, they kept on requesting more functionality and conducting more testing, putting off the go-live date several times because they were uncertain whether they would be able to operate their business on the new system. The project continued—significantly over budget and well past rescheduled due dates—and still the system was not completed. Eventually, the project was abandoned and the UK software firm was never able to make inroads into Asia.

A Fish Out of Water

The Western-based consulting firms first arrived in Asia often in response to the needs of their existing, home market–based global clients—assigning Western partners to help develop their Asian practice. An immediate challenge they faced is that a large number of the global consulting firms are limited in terms of ethnic and cultural diversity within their home market ranks. The assigned partners, even those with some international travel under their belts, are usually unprepared for the differences in the business, educational, and cultural environments in a region like Asia. Once on the ground, it takes time for a Western partner to build the networks, adapt their personal style, and begin to understand how to sell and deliver consulting effectively in Asia.

Focus on the Western Buyers

The easiest client targets for consulting firms that are trying to build practices in Asia are Western executives of multinational corporations. They know that these executives understand the potential role of consultants and thus are more open to using them. They also assume, often correctly, that these executives are highly influenced by the brand image of global consulting firms based on their own or colleagues' experiences with the brand in the Western home markets.

We have seen that the primary sales approach of global consulting firms setting up in Asia is to (a) build up the relationship with Western expatriates; (b) market and build trust in the brand by handing over surveys, studies, and thought pieces written in the United States; (c) bring in a partner from North America or Europe with industry eminence to lead a free workshop, brainstorming session, or idea-validation session; (d) back up any proposal with an extensive list of previous clients, few or none of which are in the country—or even the region—or involved any members of the proposed team; and (e) embed a "fly-in" advisory partner in the proposed team who has done exactly the same project for a North American or European client.

As the potential buyer, you should not underestimate how hard it is to create a consistent "product" around the globe, relying on consulting firms to deliver teams of human resources drawn from the local talent pool. And although the eminent advisory partner will be a very high-cost component of the overall proposal, if they have not spent much time in Asia, they are unlikely to be very effective. They do not understand how to apply solutions in Asia, and the local staff, although respectful, will not listen to them because they know that the fly-in partner will not stick around long enough to help make them successful.

As case study A1.2 illustrates, though the exotic foreign assignment may appear alluring at first, it quickly becomes a chore for the consultants who must regularly travel to destinations where partners have sold a project, but which they personally have no interest in or long-term commitment to.

Case Study A1.2
FOREIGN COUNTRY ASSIGNMENT CHALLENGES DESTROY VALUE

A company in Japan was looking for consulting support in an area that was quite specialized to their industry. Rather than hire a local consulting firm they had worked with before (but whose team for this particular assignment they were not acquainted with), they flew in a team of consultants from overseas. These consultants, while knowledgeable in their subject area, had no grounding in Japan and no local office to draw support from. Travel fatigue and culture shock soon set in: the team members became sick, refused to travel within Japan, failed to gather the relevant fact base, and alienated all of the company's Japanese employees. The project did not produce any actionable results, and though desperately needing attention, the whole division became a no-go area for consultants due to the trauma inflicted on them by the unwittingly insensitive overseas experts.

Pyramids Take Time to Build

If you recall, mature consulting practices have a pyramid of partners, directors/senior managers, managers, senior consultants, and consultants. It takes many years to develop a strong complement of resources at each level. Consulting firms in Asia must develop the talent pool and build the consulting resource pyramid within their defined practices. Yet the "global" training courses are devised by the consulting firms based on the educational background and cultural tendencies of Western consultants. As a result, there are many misalignments in sequence, content, and delivery approach in the training curriculum that make it difficult to simply implement them in Asia.

Even if the training curriculum is comprehensive and relevant to Asia, the on-the-job acquisition of skills and experiences that allows progress from consultant to partner normally takes more than ten years. One way to shortcut the time it takes to populate the higher pyramid levels is to make senior hires. Thus, global consulting firms hire senior managers in Asia, usually from the industry sectors they are focused on, who have the potential to become future practice leaders. They expect to be able to leverage the strong industry relationships of these local senior managers to generate sales opportunities and corresponding revenue for the fledging consulting practice. Unfortunately, these senior managers rarely make a successful transition into true consulting professionals given their distaste for hands-on, detailed work that is considered beneath them. Therefore, they fail to learn how to do lower-level analytical tasks and to solve problems using structured techniques.

In terms of the junior consultants, local candidates are enthusiastic about the opportunities to learn and work within international companies, and they readily accept job offers from consulting firms. But they often have unrealistic expectations about promotions and titles, quickly becoming impatient with a three-year cycle and the need to spend years, not months, at each level before progressing to the next. They look for opportunities in competing firms that attract them with the promise of an instant promotion.

You, as the buyer, must ascertain how many years of actual consulting experience every proposed team member has, including the partners and senior managers. The consulting experience represents the value to you; just because a consultant was employed by one of your competitors until recently does not mean that you will be able to replicate your competitor's success. Also, you should negotiate billing rates if you believe that the proposed consultants do not have the experience and expertise consistent with their title.

Case study A1.3 illustrates the poor value realized for both the consulting firm and their client when revenue pressure on consulting partners is combined with the immature consulting capabilities in Asia.

Case Study A1.3

REVENUE PRESSURES AND IMMATURE CAPABILITY DRIVE PROJECT FAILURE

The Asian division of a global consulting firm had an opportunity to implement a new enterprise resource planning system for a financial services company in a country in Asia. However, the country managing partner, a Westerner, was not knowledgeable about the technology, and the recently hired senior manager responsible for the proposal was focused on getting a sale regardless of how unprofitable the project or unrealistic the commitment to the client might be. The relatively low proposal amount that he came up with meant that the regional office risk and pricing review was not required by the consulting firm before the bid was submitted. Not surprisingly, the consulting firm won the bid on price, which at a low fixed fee was highly attractive to the client.

Within several months of executing the multiyear project, the consulting firm's resource costs exceeded the fixed-fee amount, at which point the project triggered a risk review by the regional office. It was apparent that the work had been significantly underpriced; there had been considerable miscommunication between the client and the consultant as to how many phases of the multiphase implementation were included in the fixed fee; and the manager assigned to the project (the senior manager had since left the firm) had done an abysmal job of managing the scope of the engagement.

The consulting firm decided that it would be better to simply withdraw from the project at the end of the current phase than to try to get the client to agree to pay more fees for the subsequent phases. The client top executive, who would lose face if the consulting firm that he had selected withdrew (not to mention having to deal with the issues that a project delay would cause), was incensed, and he threatened to blacklist the consulting firm if they pursued this course of action. Eventually, through their respective lawyers, the global consulting firm managed to negotiate a withdrawal.

The consulting firm repaid the fees earned, fired several of the staff, and implemented much stricter pricing policies and controls. The client restarted the project with another consulting firm, realizing that the low fixed fee they had originally accepted had not been such a bargain after all.

English Fluency Is Not Enough

Demand is high for the senior English-speaking Asian national who has been educated in the West. This individual can virtually dictate their compensation package. Unfortunately, many Westerners make the mistake of equating English language skills with technical capabilities. There is simply no correlation. Consulting firms are no exception. They hire mid-career staff because of their language capabilities, hoping that the consultant's grasp of English will compensate for lack of any competency that could form the foundation of a consulting career.

As a potential client, do not assume that the English speakers are as competent at consulting as they are at English. And do not simply reject non-English-speaking but otherwise capable consultants just because you are not able to personally converse with them.

Fragmentation Inhibits Critical Mass

Of all the countries in Asia, only Japan and, more recently, South Korea have had the economic scale, thanks to a large pipeline of client revenue, to develop and sustain full-service consulting practices. This has allowed them to staff projects across a broad array of industry and functional disciplines. But it is not easy to effectively utilize consultants from Japan and South Korea on projects elsewhere in Asia, since too few speak another Asian language or English. Companies in Asia must also be aware that it is more difficult for Asian consultants to work around Asia than for Europeans to operate across Europe. For example, it is problematic to assign Japanese consultants to a project in China or to have ethnically Chinese consultants work in Indonesia due to language barriers and/or historical cross-cultural perceptions.

The economies of most other countries in Asia are either still too small or at too early a stage of development to generate the constant stream of sizable projects that drive the demand for consulting services, and which consulting firms need to build critical mass. Thus, client projects are usually staffed with consultants who tend to be generalists when compared to the specialists that Western consultants have become, and who are less trained and experienced than their counterparts in North America and Europe even though their titles may be the same and the rates at which they are billed are often equivalent.

Organizations hiring consultants in Asia must confirm that the proposed team includes a large enough proportion of staff from within the relevant country; otherwise, the consultants will be incapable of penetrating the veneer of your organization. They will not be able to build rapport with your team, understand the nuances of the information they provided, or convince your staff that their proposals are workable within your company's and country's unique business environment.

Continuity Is Challenging

Very few Western partners are willing to spend the years in Asia that are required to build a robust consulting practice. Thus, a succession of these Western partners is continually grappling with the learning curve, recovering from cultural gaffes, and realizing that Asia is not a country, or even a continent, and that it doesn't have a common language. As a result, each new partner is inevitably building or rebuilding consulting practices virtually from scratch. The capabilities of consulting practices of the various global consulting firms rise and fall with the movement of their partners. The vast majority of consulting firms, irrespective of whether they focus on strategy, process, or technology, have had numerous false starts in their attempts to build their consulting practices in Asia.

So, to the savvy buyer of consulting services, consulting firms' qualifications are even less relevant in Asia, even if the referenced clients are in Asia. There is a good chance that the entire team that worked on the referenced assignment will no longer be employed by the consulting firm a year or two after completion. And just because you received high-quality services from a consulting firm on an engagement last year, there is no guarantee that you will receive the same standard on another engagement next year.

Demand Outstrips Supply

Despite all of the forgoing, the fact remains that there is more demand for consulting services in Asia than there is supply of qualified consultants. Within that context, some consulting firms can afford to be inflexible because they are confident they can secure work and premium rates from other less educated and less demanding clients. If your organization is a global strategic account for the consulting firm, you may have more negotiating leverage. It also helps to have the consulting firm invest a lot of effort to secure your business, which makes it more difficult for them to walk away from it in favor of an easier sell elsewhere.

Given the lack of bench strength and depth within the Asia-based offices of global management consulting firms, independent consultants or small local consulting practices have much greater relative impact in Asia than elsewhere. However, you need to ensure that the consultants you select are sufficiently well rounded to meet your requirements.

Buyer Beware

Given the challenges of diverse educational foundations, unprepared transitory Western partners, senior managers in Asia who do not build the necessary depth of skills, the difficulty in developing and retaining junior consultants, the lack of appropriate training curriculum from the global practice, and the fragmented character of the region conspiring against achieving critical mass, it should be no surprise that very few of the "global" consulting firms have been able to build sustainable practices with the necessary breadth and depth of consultants to provide value for their clients.

If you are part of an organization with interests in Asia, you will have to exert far more effort to assure yourself that value is available from prospective consulting firms than you would have to in their more established Western-based practices.

Management Summary

- The origins of the management consulting profession are based first in North America, and second in Europe. The profession is emerging in Asia.

- Global management consulting firms have had difficulty building sustainable practices comparable in quality to those in North America due to their short-term management horizons and the broader cultural differences in Asia.

- Western consulting partners who have little experience in Asia are usually not conscious of the differences in cultural tendencies and have difficulty judging the quality of hires. It can be a challenge for them to deliver value in Asia.

- Avoid basing decisions in Asia on the global brand; you must vet capabilities at the individual consultant level.

- Recognize that competent consultants in the areas you require may simply not be available in some countries in Asia. When working on large projects, you may need to configure the resources from multiple sources rather than rely on a single consulting firm.

- Verify how well the consulting firm has adapted their approach to your country by ascertaining how many of the consultants speak the local language, what training the Western consultants have received on local cultural norms, and how the consulting internal training programs are adapted for your country.

- It is very much buyer beware in Asia, with title inflation, fragmentation of expertise, little bench strength, and demand overwhelming supply—all of which results in high variability in capability and delivery performance throughout the region.

- Contractually ensure that the resources proposed and which you vetted are actually committed to your project and will not be substituted after the consulting firm has won the business. As the bench strength for any consulting firm is weak in Asia, it is unlikely the substitute will be as qualified as the initially proposed resource.

- Understand that the experiences of individual consultants are likely to be less than their titles suggest. Be sure you pay for capabilities, not titles.

STRUCTURE OF A TYPICAL RFP

THE STRUCTURE BELOW IS TYPICAL OF A REQUEST FOR PROPOSAL (RFP) for advisory and implementation services. It shows more detail than what would be included when pure advisory services, such as strategy consulting, are sought. At the other extreme, an RFP for outsourcing services would require more information, particularly on the post-implementation state, such as service levels, business continuity, and charging structures. The selection of other products (software, technology) and services (accounting, legal, banking) are beyond the scope of this book and would require that more technical information be provided and collected than what is required for consulting services. Figure A2.1 represents a balance across the spectrum of consulting services and should provide a starting point for most RFPs.

Figure A2.1: Structure of a Typical RFP

Purpose	Chapter
Company and RFP Background	1 This Request for Proposal 2 Introduction to the Company

Problem Statement and Definition of Success	3 Current State, Vision, and Design Principles
	   3.1 Organization and Processes
	   3.2 Systems and Technology Infrastructure
	4 Detailed Business Objectives and Requirements

Consulting Services and Roles Required	5 Scope of Services to Be Included in the Proposal
	   5.1 Project Strategy, Structure, and Timeline
	   5.2 Project Geographic and Business Scope
	   5.3 Scope
	   5.4 Services and Roles Required

Pricing Proposition	6 Pricing Structure
	   6.1 Pricing Approach
	   6.2 Fee Breakdown Requirements
	   6.3 Bonus/Penalty Arrangements
	   6.4 Expense and Travel Guidelines
	   6.5 The Company's Standard Consulting Contract

Format for proposal to ensure that all proposals have the same information and can easily be compared side by side	7 Required Proposal Contents
	   7.1 Project Assumptions
	   7.2 Projected Measurable Benefits
	   7.3 Delivery of Services
	        7.3.1 Project Approach
	        7.3.2 Project Plan and Milestones
	        7.3.3 Project Management
	        7.3.4 Consulting Firm's Responsibilities and Deliverables
	        7.3.5 Consultant's Expectations of the Company
	        7.3.6 Project Location and Facilities
	        7.3.7 Approach to Disengagement
	   7.4 Consultant's Perspectives
	   7.5 Contract Structure and Terms
	        7.5.1 Contract Architecture
	        7.5.2 Contracting Approach
	        7.5.3 Response to the Company's Contract Terms
	        7.5.4 Sample Consulting Firm Contract

Purpose	Chapter
	7.6 Pricing Structure
	7.6.1 Total Fees and Assumptions for Fees
	7.6.2 Detailed Fees and Effort
	7.6.3 Bonus/Penalty Payments
	7.6.4 Consultant Rate Structure
	7.6.5 Expense and Travel Policy
	7.7 Consulting Firm's Credentials
	7.7.1 Proposed Consultants and Their Project Role
	7.7.2 Consultant Résumés
	7.7.3 Matrix of Consultants and Referenced Clients
	7.8 Suitability as a Service Provider
	7.8.1 Conflicts of Interest
	7.8.2 Degree of Concentration on Work Proposed
	7.8.3 Other Disclosures
	7.9 Consulting Firm's Approach to Risk
	7.9.1 Implementation Risks
	7.9.2 Preventative Assurance
	7.9.3 Contingency Arrangements
	7.9.4 Remedies Available in the Event of Nonperformance
	7.9.5 Insurance Coverage
How you will work with the consultant	8 The Company's Expectations of Consultants
	8.1 Cooperative Arrangements
	8.2 Consultant's Contractual Responsibilities
	8.3 Consultant's Conduct
	8.4 Language Requirements
Clearly defined process and timeline for the RFP	9 Proposal Process
	9.1 Selection Criteria
	9.2 Selection Timeline
	9.3 Intention to Propose
	9.4 The Company Contact Person
	9.5 Questions
	9.6 Submission of Proposal
	9.7 Consultant Presentations
	9.8 Follow-up
	9.9 Contract Negotiations
	9.10 Disposal of Confidential Information

Purpose	Chapter
	10 Proposal Conditions and Requirements
	10.1 Unfair Advantage
	10.2 Right Not to Proceed
	10.3 Right to Negotiate
	10.4 Proposal Conformance
	10.5 Changes to the RFP
	10.6 Proposal Retention and Ownership
	10.7 Cost of Proposal
	10.8 Misleading or False Information
	10.9 Disclaimer
	10.10 Confidentiality
	10.11 Third-Party Disclosure and News Releases

KEY COMPONENTS OF A CONSULTING CONTRACT

FIGURE A3.1 LISTS THE KEY HEADINGS FOR TERMS THAT SHOULD, AT a minimum, be covered in any consulting services contract. You should recognize that actual terms are subject to negotiation and that the standard terms will vary from jurisdiction to jurisdiction.

Figure A3.1: Key Components of a Consulting Contract

Section	Key Headings
Construction of Agreement	Definitions Attached Documents Precedence of Documents Entire Agreement Severability Waivers
Services	Scope of Services Responsibilities Deliverables Contract Term Quality Assurance

Section	Key Headings
Resources	Resources Exclusivity Resource Substitution Resource Continuity Use of Subcontractors Standard of Care Cooperation with Third Parties
Commercial Terms	Overall Fee Rates Rate Escalation Expense and Travel Policy Invoicing Procedures Payment Terms Audit Rights
IP and Confidentiality	Intellectual Property Personal Data Privacy Confidentiality Ownership of Deliverables
Termination	Termination by Client Termination by Consultant Notice Period Transition Assistance
Competition	Nonsolicitation of Personnel Noncompete
Guarantees	Liability Warranty Insurance Indemnity

Section	Key Headings
Other	Dispute Resolution
	Governing Law
	Limitation on Actions
	Force Majeure
	Assignment
	Survival
	Independent Contractor
	Escalation
	Notices
	Changes to the Agreement

ORGANIZATION EVALUATION

Procurement Function

1. Is there a central consultant procurement function or an internal control-and-review process in place to ensure that a formal selection process is used to find the most capable and cost-effective consultant for the project? *Yes No*

2. Is there a formal approach to internally define the problem before obtaining the perspectives of the various candidate consulting firms? *Yes No*

3. Do you have a well-defined approach for developing an RFI and an RFP—including documenting the selection criteria—as well as the process for managing both? *Yes No*

4. Do you have predefined contract terms and an expense policy to provide to the consulting firms with an RFP? *Yes No*

Selection

5. Did you expand the list of potential candidate consulting firms through the use of third-party evaluators such as Gartner, Foresters, or IDC? *Yes No*

6. Did you undertake an Internet search on the consulting partners and other personnel presented to you to determine their actual interests and expertise based on their articles, presentations, and news releases? *Yes No*

7. Did you validate the reality of the capabilities of each key consultant being proposed for your project relative to their assigned roles? *Yes No*

8. Did you ensure that the proposed consultants will be contracted to the project for the appropriate amount of time during the project? *Yes No*

9. Did you analyze the merits of the proposals (capability to deliver) before evaluating the commercial relationships? *Yes No*

10. Did the business sponsor of the project actively participate with the company's legal counsel during the contracting process? *Yes No*

11. Did you document the business outcome, target metrics, the current baseline for the target metrics, and measurement approach, and did this document form a part of the contract with the consulting firm? *Yes No*

Management

12. Were the consultant's terms of reference for their engagement appropriately aligned to support the achievement of the business objectives of your project? *Yes No*

13. Was a project manager assigned from within your organization to manage or work in tandem with the consulting firm's engagement manager? *Yes No*

14. Did you make sure the logistics were attended to so that the consultants could be productive from day one? *Yes* *No*

15. Did the project team integrate personnel from your organization and the consulting firm, taking care to minimize the absolute number of consultants and the ratio of consultants to your internal team members? *Yes* *No*

16. Did you assign high-quality people from your organization to the project team? *Yes* *No*

17. Did the consulting firm's partner and project manager provide regular updates on progress and findings? *Yes* *No*

18. Did you identify any telltale signs that would indicate your project may be in trouble? *Yes* *No*

19. Were you in control of the consultants all of the time? *Yes* *No*

Release

20. Have you confirmed the receipt and location of the full inventory of electronic and hard-copy versions of working, interim, and final documents left behind? *Yes* *No*

21. Have you reviewed the consultant's deliverables against those originally promised and agreed upon in their contract and proposal documents? *Yes* *No*

22. Have you confirmed the realization of business objectives and target metrics or—if too early—the management process and timing to monitor their realization? *Yes* *No*

23. Have multiple employees within your organization received full knowledge transfer from the consultants, and will they be able to operate independently when the consultants have gone? *Yes* *No*

24. Have you conducted a debriefing among your employees focused on lessons learned from their use of consultants? *Yes* *No*

25. Have you asked the consulting firm to warrant that they have returned or disposed of all confidential or proprietary materials provided to them? *Yes No*

26. Have you debriefed with your internal consulting services procurement function? *Yes No*

27. Have you entered your experience with the consulting firm, including rate structures and man hours, onto:

    a. Your organization's knowledge base so that other authorized personnel can access it? *Yes No*

    b. The website www.ExtractValueFromConsultants.com so you can benchmark your organization's processes for extracting value from consultants with other organizations? *Yes No*

APPENDIX 5

CONSULTANT EVALUATION

1. Background
   1.1 Name of consulting firm _____
   1.2 Name of partner/principal _____
   1.3 Name of project manager _____
   1.4 Geographic location of the engagement _____
   1.5 Total contracted fees (US$) _____
   1.6 Total contract days _____
   1.7 Duration of the engagement _____

2. What was the nature of your project?
   a. Change management
   b. Corporate strategy
   c. Operational strategy
   d. Process redesign
   e. Systems implementation
   f. Technology infrastructure
   g. Other _____

3. How did you identify the consulting firm that could address your requirements?
   a. Corporate vendor list
   b. Incumbent
   c. Internet search
   d. Marketing (advertising, article, book, magazine, conference presentation)
   e. Personal relationship
   f. Recent sales call
   g. Referred by trusted source
   h. Third-party reviewer
   i. Well-known brand
   j. Other _____

4. How many consulting firms did you invite to bid on your RFP?

   _____

5. What tactics, if any, did the selected consulting firm employ during the selection process?
   a. Changed nature of project
   b. Followed process outlined in the RFP
   c. Influenced decision makers
   d. Influenced superiors
   e. Provided free services
   f. Other _____

6. How well did the chosen consulting firm follow your selection process?
   Not at all   *Completely*

   0   1   2   3   4   5   6   7   8   9   10

7. How closely did your actual experience reflect the capabilities of the consultants represented during the proposal process?
   Not at all accurate   *Perfect match*

   0   1   2   3   4   5   6   7   8   9   10

8. How flexible was your consultant during the contracting process?

    Insisted on their terms   *Agreed to all our terms*

    0 1 2 3 4 5 6 7 8 9 10

9. To what extent did your consultant pursue their own firm's objectives versus your project's business objectives?

    Consulting firm objectives   *Organization project objectives*

    0 1 2 3 4 5 6 7 8 9 10

10. How successful do you consider the project to have been?

    Failure   *Exceeded expectations*

    0 1 2 3 4 5 6 7 8 9 10

11. What is the probability of you using this consulting firm again?

    Never   *Definitely*

    0 1 2 3 4 5 6 7 8 9 10

12. What percentage of the original contract price did the fees for subsequent scope changes account for?_____

13. Did you award the consultant any follow-on work?

    a. Yes, continuation into next phase of the project
    b. Yes, on an unrelated project, without a new selection process
    c. Yes, on an unrelated project but with a new selection process
    d. No

Other comments about your experience with the consulting firm with whom you worked. _____

_____

_____

_____

BIBLIOGRAPHY

Books, Journals & Reports

Hofstede, G. 1997. *Cultures and Organizations: Software of the Mind* (McGraw-Hill).

Hofstede, G. 2001. *Cultures Consequences: International Differences in Work-Related Values* (Sage).

Huijser, M. 2006. *The Culture Advantage* (Intercultural Press).

Longwood, J., and F. Ng. 2008. *Market Overview: Consulting and SI Service Providers, Asia/Pacific* (Gartner Group).

Lewis, R.D. 1996. *When Cultures Collide* (Nicholas Brealey Publishing).

Mackay, A. 2006. *Recruiting, Retaining & Releasing People: Managing Redeployment, Return, Retirement and Redundancy* (Elsevier Science and Technology books).

Mathews, K., A. Newton, and D. Smith. 2009. *Report Summary, Global Consulting Marketplace 2009–2012: Key Trends, Profiles and Forecasts* (Kennedy Consulting Research & Advisory).

McKenna, C.D. 2006. *The World's Newest Profession* (Cambridge University Press).

Minto, B. 1996. *The Minto Pyramid Principle: Logic in Writing, Thinking and Problem Solving* (Minto International, Inc.).

Smith, D. 2007. *Report Summary, Global Consulting Marketplace 2007–2010: Key, Trends, Profiles and Forecasts* (Kennedy Information).

Unlisted Author. 2008. *User Survey Analysis: U.S. Business Consulting; What Customers Want and What Providers Must Do in 2008* (Gartner Group).

Consulting Firm Websites

Accenture, www.accenture.com

Arthur D. Little, www.arthurdlittle.com

AT Kearney, www.atkearney.com

Atos Origin, www.atosorigin.com

Bain & Company, www.bain.com

BearingPoint, www.bearingpoint.com

Booz & Company, www.booz.com

Booz Allen Hamilton, www.boozallen.com

Boston Consulting Group, www.bcg.com

Cap Gemini, www.capgemini.com

Computer Sciences Corporation (CSC), www.csc.com

Deloitte, www.deloitte.com

Electronic Data Systems (EDS), www.eds.com

Ernst & Young, www.ey.com

Fujitsu Consulting, www.fujitsu.com/global

IBM Consulting, www-935.ibm.com/services/us/gbs/bus/html/bcs_index.html

Infosys, www.infosys.com

KPMG, www.kpmg.com

Logica, www.logica.com

McKinsey & Company, www.mckinsey.com

Monitor Group, www.monitor.com

Oliver Wyman, www.oliverwyman.com

PA Consulting Group, www.paconsulting.com

PricewaterhouseCoopers, www.pwc.com

Roland Berger, www.rolandberger.com

S&T Consulting, www.snt-world.com

Steria Consulting, www.steria.com

Tata Consultancy Services, www.tcs.com

Towers Perrin, www.towersperrin.com

Xansa, www.xansa.com

INDEX